to
think

Other books by Frank Smith:

The Genesis of Language: A Psycholinguistic Approach (edited, with George A. Miller) (1966)

Psycholinguistics and Reading (1973)

Comprehension and Learning: A Conceptual Framework (1975)

Writing and the Writer (1982)

Essays into Literacy: Selected Papers and Some Afterthoughts (1983)

Awakening to Literacy (edited, with Hillel Goelman and Antoinette A. Oberg) (1984)

Reading Without Nonsense, Second Edition (1985)

Insult to Intelligence (1986)

Joining the Literacy Club (1987)

Understanding Reading, Fourth Edition (1988)

to
think

Frank Smith

Teachers College, Columbia University
New York and London

Published by Teachers College Press, 1234 Amsterdam Avenue
New York, NY 10027

Library of Congress Cataloging-in-Publication Data

Smith, Frank, 1928–
  To think / Frank Smith.
      p.   cm.
  Includes bibliographical references and index.
  ISBN 0-8077-3062-9 (alk. paper). — ISBN 0-8077-3057-2 (pbk. :
alk. paper)
  1. Critical thinking. I. Title.
BC177.S59   1990
153.4'2—dc20   90-41901

ISBN 0-8077-3062-9
ISBN 0-8077-3057-2 (pbk.)

Printed on acid-free paper
Manufactured in the United States of America
97 96 95 94 93 92 91 90 8 7 6 5 4 3 2 1

CONTENTS

PREFACE   VII

1   TALKING ABOUT THINKING   1
Thinking—In Seventy-Seven Words   1
What the Words Refer To   2
Making a Mystery of Thinking   5
The Language of this Book   8

2   COMMONPLACE THINKING   12
The Business of the Brain   13
Making Decisions   15
Problem-Solving   17
Reasoning   19
Formal and Informal Logic   21
"Higher-Order Thinking"   23
Easy and Difficult Thinking   27

3   REMEMBERING, UNDERSTANDING, AND LEARNING   32
Remembering   33
Understanding   35
Learning   37
Remembering, Understanding, Learning, and Thinking   43

4   IMAGINATION   45
Creating Reality   45
Realities of the Imagination   48
Specifications of Imagination   49
Imagination, Remembering, Understanding, and Learning   50
Imagination and Thinking   52
The Dynamo of the Brain   53

5   PATTERNS AND STORIES   55
Imposing Order on Visual Chaos   55
Other Patterns   59

Patterns in Time   61
The Stories Behind Thought   62
Other Realities   66

6 THINKING CREATIVELY   72
Talking About Creativeness   73
The Experience of Art   78
The Creation of Art   82

7 THINKING CRITICALLY   91
Talking About Critical Thinking   91
Aspects of Critical Thinking   95
How to Think Critically   102

8 THINKING AND LANGUAGE   108
What Thought Does   109
What Language Does   110
Language and Stories   112
Thought and Language   115
The Reclusiveness of Thought   118
Thought and the Brain   120

9 THINKING AND EDUCATION   124
Facilitating Thinking   126
Interfering with Thinking   128
Improving Thinking in Schools   129
The Need to Think   131
Who's Right?   133

NOTES   135

REFERENCES   163

INDEXES   175

ABOUT THE AUTHOR   181

PREFACE

My purpose in writing this book is an exercise of its theme, to think about what it means to think. Examining the way people think, and the reasons they think the way they do, seems to me at least as interesting and important as understanding the working of digestive systems, governments, or computers.

I am also concerned by a widespread perception of a decline or inadequacy in ability to think, usually coupled with pronouncements that something should be done about the situation. Some people would like to be able to "think better"—or more often they want other people's thinking to improve. There are frequent complaints that students of all ages—and children and adults out of school—are defective thinkers. The anxiety is misplaced, and unthinking attempts to teach "thinking skills" can discriminate against many students, persuading them that they are incapable of thinking, a view that their teachers may too readily adopt.

Calls for educational action imply that problems with thinking result from a lack of appropriate instruction. Yet innumerable research studies during the past thirty years, and centuries of common observation, confirm that, with rare and obvious exceptions, everyone is born capable of thinking. Infants have exquisitely efficient brains that they use with inconspicuous competence to learn about the world, culture, social structure, and language into which they are born, largely without formal instruction of any kind. Babies think, and think very well.

If we were all such powerful thinkers as infants, do we lose this ability as we get older? Or is infant thinking irrelevant to school and the grown-up world? Do unschooled adults think like babies—or would we all be better off if we could think with the clarity of infancy? What kinds of thinking might have to be taught, and in what circumstances would they best be learned? What is thinking, anyway? Are there different kinds of thinking, some innate and others that must be taught? Is something lacking in the way many people think most of the time? To what extent is thinking socially determined? If schools currently teach in ways that preclude or hamper the development of thinking, how can anyone be sure that deliberate efforts to teach thinking—presumably in the thoughtless way teaching has hitherto been done—will not make matters worse? Some people may argue that there is no time to ponder such questions; the situation is urgent and immediate action must be taken. But if we never think about thinking, how can we anticipate what might be done in the name of teaching thinking?

There are some profound difficulties. Thought cannot be inspected directly, the way a scientist might examine the operations of a mechanical device or of organs such as the lungs or stomach. Research studies may demonstrate that certain areas of the brain are implicated in particular kinds of thought—for example, by being highly activated when a person is reading—but such studies can say nothing of what a person might be reading, or whether the reading is worthwhile. Physiologists may have a rough idea of *where* particular kinds of knowledge may be represented in the brain, but they cannot show *how* they are represented—how barrages of nerve impulses and tides of chemical change might carry a meaning like "I would like to visit Paris next year," as opposed to "I wanted to go to Tokyo last year." The passage of a thought through the brain cannot be traced and analyzed like the passage of food through the digestive system, and it is unclear what could be learned by such analysis that is not already apparent from the way thought is expressed.

We cannot look into other people's heads to see if they can speak French, dislike artichokes, or have an interest in computers, but we can get a good idea from the way they behave and talk. And we can only examine our own thinking in the same detached way. We cannot look into our own head to inspect our skills, likes, or interests. We have to see what we can do and prefer to do.

Despite this stubborn resistance of the brain to on-site inspection, every language is rich with terms suggesting different kinds of activities within the brain. This is the second fundamental problem—that language can paint improbably lush landscapes and ensnare us in tangled undergrowth. There are words for seemingly innumerable kinds of mental activity, as diverse as *deciding* and *imagining, remembering* and *planning,* but do they refer to different kinds of activity in the brain, or simply to different kinds of external situations or products of thought? It is a common propensity to *reify* such terms—to suppose that because a particular word exists, whatever that word refers to must also have a unique existence. Many psychological and educational assertions assume that every word in the language related to thinking must refer to a distinctive process in the brain. Language, which can (I hope) do so much to help us think about thinking, can also add to the confusion.

One of the main contentions of this book is that much philosophizing about thinking has been misled by everyday language.

There are other problems. Thinking and learning to think are commonly regarded as essentially intellectual. But thinking and learning inevitably involve feelings, and the way in which a person thinks may be primarily determined by emotional or personality considerations rather than by intellectual ability. Thinking and learning are also social activities, and most of us are greatly influenced by the way other people expect us to think and to behave. Past experience can have more bearing on what we think than present circumstances. The manner in which individuals think on particular occasions is more than a simple matter of whether appropriate skills have been properly taught.

Thinking always tends to be an emotional topic. There is a tendency to regard the thought of people who think differently from us as impaired, while our own thinking is not. And if other people do not think as we do, we tend to think that education, or better information, should put matters right. Flaws in our own thinking are almost by definition rarely apparent to us, certainly not until after the event, including those occasions when we think about thinking, our own and other people's.

Criticisms of the way students think tend naturally to what the brain is supposed to do badly, emphasizing slips and omissions while ignoring everything the brain does well. It is assumed that very little thinking is done by most people in the course of the day and that any thinking that is done is unskilled. I propose an alternative point of view: that everyday thinking—what I call *commonplace* thinking—is continually complex and extremely skillful.

Preview

Chapter 1, "Talking about Thinking," is about language, or at least those parts of language that refer to thinking. The aim is to clarify what all the words that are related to thinking might tell us about thought, or how they might confound and confuse us. Chapter 2, "Commonplace Thinking," examines everyday aspects of thinking and how they are accomplished much more effectively than we usually give ourselves or other people credit for. Chapter 3, "Remembering, Understanding, and Learning," considers other commonplace aspects of everyday mental life, showing that they are inseparable from thinking in general, and consistently much more efficient than we usually believe.

Chapter 4 looks at "Imagination," another persistent and underrated aspect of everyday thinking, which I argue energizes and directs everything the brain does. Chapter 5, "Patterns and Stories," focuses on our continual construction and recognition of patterns in experience, keeping the imagination relevant and efficacious. Chapter 6 and Chapter 7, on "Thinking Creatively" and "Thinking Critically," look at aspects of thinking often thought to be difficult, distinctive, and significant, and find them not to be so very different after all.

Language is much more than a vehicle for talking about thinking, of course. It is itself an expression of thinking and in its turn has an undoubted influence on thought. Chapter 8, "Thinking and Language," examines these complex and important relationships. Finally, Chapter 9, "Thinking and Education," is concerned with how thinking might be improved, especially in educational contexts.

Acknowledgments and Notes to each of the chapters appear before the References at the end of the book.

1

TALKING ABOUT THINKING

Words are clues to the things people believe to be important. Societies that regard horses, or snow, or clouds, as significant parts of their lives, for example, have a multiplicity of words for different kinds of horses, snow, or clouds. On this basis, thinking must be a major concern of speakers of English. There is a sea of words that refer to thinking—and it will be useful to scan the semantic horizon before plunging in.

THINKING—IN SEVENTY-SEVEN WORDS

Here is a brief and incomplete list of English verbs related to thinking:

analyze	conjecture	fabricate	organize
anticipate	consider	fantasize	plan
apprehend	contemplate	foresee	plot
argue	create	guess	ponder
assert	deduce	hypothesize	postulate
assume	deem	imagine	predict
attend	deliberate	induce	premeditate
believe	determine	infer	presume
calculate	devise	intend	presuppose
categorize	discover	introspect	project
classify	divine	invent	propose
cogitate	empathize	judge	rationalize
comprehend	estimate	know	reason
conceive	examine	meditate	recall
concentrate	expect	muse	reflect
conceptualize	explain	opine	remember

review	scheme	suspect	wonder
revise	speculate	systematize	
ruminate	suggest	theorize	
schematize	suppose	understand	

The list is illustrative, not exhaustive. I have deliberately excluded uncommon or exotic words like *animadvert, brood, fancy, hazard, lucubrate, soliloquize, trow,* and *ween.* And I have also left out some words that might in particular contexts imply thinking—such as *exploring, outlining,* and *sketching*—and a host of others that relate to more conspicuous activities, like reading and writing, although thinking must certainly be at the heart of them.

There are many ways in which my seventy-seven "thinking" words could be organized, apart from the rather unimaginative (unthinking?) alphabetical order that I have employed. The words could be grouped on a temporal basis. Some look back on past events: *deduce, explain, recall, reflect, remember, review,* and *revise.* Some project into the future: *anticipate, conceive, divine, expect, foresee, imagine, intend, plan, plot, predict, project,* and *scheme.* Others seem mostly concerned with what is going on at the moment (although the present is never entirely free of past or future connotations): *analyze, argue, assert, assume, attend, believe, categorize, classify, comprehend, concentrate, conceptualize, determine, empathize, estimate, examine, invent, judge, know, opine, organize, presume, propose, reason, suggest, suspect,* and *understand.*

Some of the words seem to be anchored in the substance of actual events, like *concentrate, explain,* and *reason,* while others are more concerned with possibilities, or impossibilities, like *fantasize, imagine,* and *theorize.* Some pairs of words are opposite in meaning, such as *reason* and *guess,* or *remember* and *anticipate.* Some words suggest things done quickly, while others entail deliberation; some concern specifics and others generalities; some imply a self-evident conclusion while others indicate uncertainty. There is little that all the terms have in common—except that in sentences they can usually be replaced by the word "think" or a term like "thinking about," together with a few other words of elaboration.

WHAT THE WORDS REFER TO

The seventy-seven words also have in common the fact that they refer to things that people do. They describe activities of *people,* not of their brains. While the brain is normally regarded as the organ of thought, "thinking" words do not—except indirectly and implicitly—refer to what the brain is doing. The words all presuppose that something is going on in the brain (rather than in the liver or the lungs), but they do not specifically refer to what is going on in the brain. They refer to what the person is doing.[1]

We would not normally say that our brain is learning French, or pondering the world economy—we would say that *we* are doing those things. Even for something that transpires totally within the privacy of the head, like imagining, we would usually say that we, not our brains, are doing it. Normally I would say that "I" am remembering, considering, or feeling overwhelmed by something (just as I would normally say that I was digesting my dinner, rather than that my digestive system was doing so on my behalf). If I do say that my brain is remembering, considering, or overwhelmed by something, I am employing a figure of speech—or constructing an argument that I want to be taken as analytical and scientific. I am speaking in a special kind of context.

The seventy-seven words are all useful, and the English language would be poorer without them. Few of the words are synonymous with each other, and as I have demonstrated, some are mutually contradictory. But because English can find employment for at least seventy-seven words to make different kinds of statements about what people do when they think, it does not follow that there must be seventy-seven different kinds of thinking for the brain to do. Words are not a psychological theory, and they provide no clues to the nature of mental activity. There are scores of different words for ways of preparing and consuming meals, but not scores of different ways of digesting them.

There is usually no mystery about any of the seventy-seven words. We do not normally have to ask what they mean when we hear them in conversation, or read them in a novel. We can imagine what people are doing when the words are applied to them; we can even make assumptions about why they are doing those things, about their purposes and motivation.

If you tell me you are thinking about a meal we had together, I imagine the food that was on the table, not the mental activity that is currently occupying your brain. If you tell me that my friend George is anticipating, or arguing, or planning something, I picture him doing it. I do not picture something going on in his head, even when he is doing something utterly private and inconspicuous, like meditating or contemplating. In that case I imagine him sitting in a chair with a reflective look on his face, or something like that.

None of the "thinking" words produces an image of any kind of brain activity. In fact I have no idea what is going on in anyone's head when these various manifestations of thought are engaged in, except that it must be relevant to what the person is doing. Chemical and neural changes take place in the brain all the time, but such changes are not part of my understanding of the words. Neuroscientists scan or probe the brains of their patients in a variety of ways, but they can never see what the patients are thinking. They have no idea whether the patient is analyzing, remembering, reflecting, and so on. To find out, they have to ask the thinker, or observe the person as a whole.

We cannot even look into our own brains to see what they are doing when we think, any more than we can look into our own eyes to see what is happening when we see. But that does not make the language of thinking difficult to understand. The language of thinking is not about brains, but about people.

Part of the mystique surrounding the word *thinking* may come from the curious fact that people usually only say they are thinking when they look as though they are doing nothing at all. We will say "I'm thinking" if we are not reading, writing, cooking an omelette, watering the plants, watching television, or doing anything else which is conspicuous and self-evident. If we were doing any of those other things, that is what we would say we were doing. But that does not mean that we are not thinking if we are doing something else. On the contrary, reading, writing, cooking, and even watching television involve thinking (although we might read or watch television to avoid thinking about something else that we ought to be attending to). When something self-evident is being done, thinking is taken for granted. Even an activity that appears to be habitual, like watering the plants or walking to the corner store, requires that thought be exercised if it is to be done appropriately, and terminated at the proper time.

It is obvious that thinking must be part of all other activities, because we would never say that we are doing them and thinking as well. It would be ridiculous for me to say that I am reading and thinking, and rude for me to suggest that you should read and think, because it is assumed that the thinking will take place. In the technical language of linguistics, thinking is a *presupposition* of reading, writing, and watching television. Watering the plants presupposes thinking about watering the plants.

We might occasionally say "You should think about that book you are reading," but that would mean that the book has a particular significance (to us, at least), and we think the reader should pay additional attention to some aspects of it. We are not suggesting that the person would not normally be thinking during the reading, but that the reader should think about particular things. We might say "You should think where you are watering" when the water is going onto the floor rather than into the planter, but we would not normally say "I'd like you to water the plants and to think about where you are watering"—the thinking is presupposed; it is taken for granted.

So here is one situation when we say we are thinking—when we are not evidently doing something else. But if we are thinking, and not conspicuously doing something else, what are we actually doing? Consciously, we are imagining something we might actually be doing or have done—rehearsing a speech, remembering a movie, anticipating a meeting or a meal. Unconsciously, we are going through all the thinking that would underlie actually making a speech, watching a movie, having a meeting or a meal.

In other words, we say we are thinking when we are imagining doing something, in the head, removed from action. Otherwise we say we are doing the thing that involves the thinking. There is no difference from a thinking point of view. Doing something and thinking of doing something are inseparable. The only distinction is that when we do something conspicuously, so that other people can or could see us doing it, we are unlikely to use a thinking term, while if we do it surreptitiously, in the privacy of our own head, we call it thinking. We cannot do things without thinking, and we cannot think without contemplating doing things. Thought is action, overt or imagined.

The other confusing thing about the word *thinking* is that it is a "default term." It tends to be used in a very general and imprecise sense when we cannot think of or be bothered to use a more precise word (just as I could have written *remember* rather than *think of* in this sentence). Rather than being regarded as an impressive, high-status term, *thinking* should perhaps be relegated to the same category as the useful but very general and imprecise term *thing*. Linguists talk about such words as "place-holders." We talk about "the thing over there" when we cannot say anything more definite about whatever the thing is, or when we are postponing making a more definite statement. The same often applies when we talk about thinking, which is not a precise term, but is used in place of more specific words that are available. To inquire into the "nature" of thinking may be as pointless as asking "What is thingness?"

MAKING A MYSTERY OF THINKING

There is no mystery about what it means to think, and nothing complicated about all the different words used to describe thoughtful activities—unless you happen to be one of the many psychologists and

educators who currently have a particular interest in the topic of thinking. Many of these specialists ask—as I am asking in this book—what it
means to think. But they turn their attention from what people are
obviously doing when they are said to be thinking to what their brains
are imagined to be doing. And many of the specialists seem to take for
granted—which I do not—that distinctive brain "processes" underlie
all or many of the seventy-seven "thinking" words, and other kinds of
thinking as well. Many specialists also seem to take for granted—which
again I do not—that all the different thinking processes that they identify (or invent) are "skills," which can only be learned and improved
through instruction.[2] There also seems to be a widespread assumption,
which I shall dispute, that most people are incapable of thinking very
well.

There are many complaints from inside and outside schools about
the quality of student thinking. These complaints are venerable and
probably unanswerable. Parents for generations have been convinced
that their children are not taught as well as they were. But the complaints rest on exactly the same assumptions about thinking as those of
the educators and theorists who are trying to do something about thinking in schools. They assume that special things have to go on in the brain
in order for particular kinds of thinking to take place, and that instruction is the only means by which people can come to think better. Educators, especially when they are criticized for not doing their jobs properly, tend to see inadequacies in terms of skill deficiencies, and to see
solutions in terms of instruction. The abundant language of thinking
has led many educational theorists to believe that there are many different skills and subskills of thinking that have to be taught. The typical
educational strategy of trying to improve (and to measure) student performance by breaking down a large subject or ability into small units
that students should master one at a time will need to be looked at
critically before we get to the end of this book.

Scientists are taught a number of parsimonious precepts about not
multiplying hypotheses beyond necessity, and about the pitfalls of reifi-
cation, of assuming that a mental construct—or a word—must represent some kind of reality. Nevertheless, psychologists and other specialists have developed complex theories of thinking (and of how thinking
should be taught), seemingly based on the idea that most, if not all, of
the "thinking" words in the dictionary represent distinct mental functions, systems, or activities in the brain.

It would be equally questionable to suggest that a new process of
thinking has been discovered every time someone devises a new way of

talking about thinking. Nevertheless, as if there were not enough words related to thinking, psychologists and educators have introduced a number of new or specialized terms that refer specifically to distinctive mental activities. Words like *discover* and *inquire* are given special meaning as mental *processes* ("the discovery process," "the inquiry process"). Some psychologists even talk about *higher mental processes* (without being specific about what lower mental processes might be). All of these processes are regarded as distinctive activities of the brain, though no neurologist or brain surgeon has ever seen one.

Ugly and unnecessary words are devised for assumed mental activities, like *inferencing* (which may drive out perfectly good words like *inferring*). New or unusual terms are introduced, like *abduction* (a process of generating hypotheses), *concept-formation, decision-making, hypothesis-testing,* and *problem-solving.* Some theorists have uncritically adopted the notion that there are particular kinds of thinking that are *creative* and *critical,* while others have posited special kinds of thinking that are *lateral* or *divergent*—and even thinking that is done with only one side of the brain.

Many contemporary psychologists are particularly interested in *cognition* (in everyday language, *knowing*), and there has been a lively branch of psychology called *cognitive psychology,* concerned primarily with the way people are supposed to acquire and employ knowledge. Cognitive psychology has, however, recently been largely swallowed up by the even more exotic and esoteric discipline of *cognitive science,*[3] which includes not only psychologists, linguists, and philosophers concerned with human knowledge and thought, but also computer system designers and artificial intelligence theorists, concerned with electronic means of storing and organizing knowledge. The result has been another inrush of new words denoting different aspects of thinking. Influenced by the manner in which computers are programmed to manipulate "information," cognitive scientists have introduced terms like *cognitive structures* (which used to be called *concepts* or *ideas*), *schemes* (or *schemas* or *schemata*), *scenarios* and *strategies* (all of which are supposed to be generalized frameworks for thinking), and even *spreading activation* in the brain (which used to be called *the association of ideas*). Knowledge and ideas have themselves become homogenized into *information,* learning becomes *reception,* and speaking and writing (and teaching) become *transmission.* The computer theorists have contributed a number of their own jargon words, like *algorithms* and *heuristics* (for certain and probable ways of acquiring knowledge or solving problems), and several graphic terms like *push down storage* (for "memory"), *input/output devices* (for eyes and ears, voices and hands), and *procedures* (for schemes or strategies). They have also enthralled many psychologists and educators with the notion of *process*.

I referred to the term *process* a few paragraphs ago in relation to discovery, inquiry, and higher mental processes. But the label has become ubiquitous in educational psychology in recent years. Processes have proliferated like viruses, becoming attached to common and previously self-sufficient words without reflection or restraint. Instead of reading, the reading process is now discussed, researched, and taught. Writing has become the writing process, joining the comprehension process, the reasoning process, and a variety of other thinking processes. The change is not superficial or mere jargon. The tag of *process* takes a meaningful word out of the world and makes it another mystery in the head. Instead of being something I do with a book or magazine, reading becomes a special sequence of events in my brain. Writing is no longer something that involves a pen or a keyboard, but the activation of particular cognitive mechanisms in the brain.

Not all of the seventy-seven thinking terms have become a process— there are still a few left for anyone wanting to open up a new area of thinking research and instructional development. But there is no evident reason why some of the words have been selected as processes and the others so far ignored. No neuroscientist has yet isolated a reasoning or comprehending or even remembering process in the brain.

All these proliferating "thinking" terms are only words. And the fact that a word exists, even when it is widely and usefully used, does not mean that there is an underlying brain process, or even that it is a unique kind of skill. The words—in their everyday use—tell us what people are doing, but they say nothing about the brain. Their relevance is semantic, not psychological.

THE LANGUAGE OF THIS BOOK

One purpose of this book is to separate semantic from psychological issues, to tease out what it is the brain does that makes all these different manifestations of thought possible, and to see the relationship of instruction to thinking.

I am not going to offer a definition of the word *thinking*, or even define how I use the word. Definitions distort and constrain the use of words in language (if the definitions can be maintained, which is rare). They ignore the fact that words in everyday use—like all the words about thinking I have been examining—have a multiplicity of senses and applications, many of them overlapping to some extent. This semantic richness is not a flaw of language—it permits new and elaborate meanings to be constructed and understood. The philosopher Karl Popper argues strongly against definitions (Popper, 1976), claiming that efforts to increase precision in language result only in loss of clarity. He spurns the efforts of people who try to assert their own definitions of how words should be used. Instead, he says, we should when necessary *describe* how words are used on particular occasions. This will be the method of this book—not to add to the large and conflicting count of definitions of thinking and all its cognate terms, but to describe what people appear to be doing, and what the brain is possibly doing, when "thinking" terms are applied to them.

Pushed for a broad description, before all the analyses and examinations begin, I would declare my own view simply to be that thinking is "the business of the brain." Anything the brain does I consider to be in the domain of thinking, even those things that are done unconsciously, habitually, or instinctively. My reason for being so general and all-embracing is that I do not arbitrarily want to exclude anything from consideration or to impose a restrictive frame of reference. I shall be specific about what I consider to be conscious and unconscious aspects of thinking, but have little to say about habits, and nothing about instincts.

My conception of thinking as "the business of the brain" is close to one of the dictionary definitions of *thinking*—"the exercise of the mind." And it leads to another area of semantic and conceptual perplexity—the relationship between mind and brain.

It is not uncommon to regard the brain as an instrument or device and the mind as its product, though there are difficulties in drawing the line between what goes on in the one or the other. Do ideas exist in the mind or the brain? Is the mind a different "level" of the brain, an emergent property of the brain, or a higher level of neural organization? Is the mind a convenient but misleading fiction for what are essentially and uniquely physical processes in the brain? These questions are unanswerable, and never will be answered by debate or by research, because the distinction between mind and brain (like the classical distinction between mind and matter) is semantic. Once again we are arguing about how words are used, and words are used according to tradition, convention, idiom, and style. Words are not evidence of ultimate truth. The fact that language makes a distinction does not mean that a distinction actually exists beyond our own perceptions.

The difference between mind and brain is purely idiomatic and stylistic. The brain is what brain surgeons operate on, the chunk of physical substance in the skull. We tell people to use their brains, not their minds. We have brain fevers, and brainstorms. On the other hand, I change my mind, but not, I hope, my brain. I bear things in mind. Things out of sight are out of mind. Advertisers and propagandists manipulate minds—although they also engage in brainwashing. There are mindless acts but brainy people. We amuse ourselves with mind-benders or brainteasers. We keep things in mind but have brain power. Melodies are equally likely to be running around in the mind or in the brain (or in the head). Are emotions and feelings in the brain or in the mind (or in the heart)? These are all figures of speech—useful, meaningful, but unrelated to physiological structures or psychological processes.

There are similar kinds of problems with *wit* and *sense*, which we can have—or lose—in the singular or plural. There are even more extreme problems with *intelligence* (which we may or may not have enough of), not to mention *perspicacity* and *perspicuity*. Do these words relate to thought, to aspects of thought, or to the way thought is used? My answer, once again, is that they are just words, useful and understandable enough in everyday conversation, but totally misleading as psychological constructs.

I know (in general terms) what is meant when I am told that someone is behaving intelligently or unintelligently in certain circumstances, and even (with rather more vagueness, depending on the circumstances) if I am told that someone is intelligent or unintelligent. But I have no idea what psychologists are talking about when they define intelligence, or look for intelligence in the brain, or presume to measure it and even to assert that it *ought* to be measured, as if it is a quantity of something that people possess. (If George is occasionally unintelligent, does that mean that he lacks intelligence, or could he possess stupidity? Either alternative sounds equally reasonable to me, from a linguistic point of view, but I do not hear psychologists trying to define, locate, or measure stupidity.)

Awash in this sea of alternative terms referring to types and degrees and aspects of thinking, we must keep reminding ourselves that they are only words; they do not represent a complexity in the brain (or mind). The everyday use of words cannot be the foundation of psychological or educational theory. A shopping list of seventy-seven conventional terms, plus some extra invented ones, cannot be the basis of theoretical formulations or instructional programs. Psychological or educational tests based on such arbitrary and ill-founded conceptualizations can only be misleading and dangerous.

I use the words *mind* and *brain* when they sound right, not because I draw a distinction between the two. (And as I have already acknowledged, in a book that claims to have a scientific basis—or, at least, tries to respect scientific findings—the word *brain* will be used when in more casual circumstances *mind*, or even *the person*, would be more appropriate.) I also do not make a distinction between *thinking* and *thought*, except for stylistic reasons. I take them both to refer to the same thing.

There is one term, or rather juxtaposition of words, that I employ that is a little unusual. I have deliberately selected this expression because it *is* unusual. I wanted a way to refer to the thinking (the thought) that goes on all the time, to get us through the day. This is thinking that we are rarely aware of and that we rarely give ourselves or other people credit for. I could call this "everyday thinking," except for the possible connotation that it is not our best, that we just use it to get by, and I argue that it is normally acute and effective. I could call it "background thinking," except that I want to avoid the implication that it is not significant.

The term I have selected is *commonplace thinking*. The first reason for my choice is that the thinking I am talking about *is* commonplace; it goes on all the time, everybody does it, and it is not unusual or special in any kind of way. Second, it is, like common sense, widely shared, enabling people to understand each other's points of view, and it develops largely as a result of association with other people. Third, like the "commonplace book" that many people keep (and more used to keep) as a record of their own and other people's thoughts that are particularly compelling, it reflects an accumulation of personal experience. But especially, I wanted to choose a term that was not familiar, that people might have to stop and think about.

Commonplace thinking *is* thought, from my point of view. It is complex, fundamental, and important. For those reasons, it will be the focus of the whole of the following chapter, and the foundation of the entire book.

2
COMMONPLACE THINKING

We rarely give ourselves credit for the amount and quality of our thinking. We accuse ourselves of acting without thinking, and critics argue that many people are unable or unwilling to think. Thinking is commonly regarded as an occasional mental chore, performed when necessity arises but not a regular or favored occupation of the brain. But the brain is thinking all the time, and usually thinking very well. There can be very few moments of the day when our brain is not busy categorizing, inferring, solving problems, deciding, and engaging in other enterprises that are supposed to be components of thinking. Thinking is commonplace and usually effortless, inconspicuous, and effective. Thinking is the way the brain arranges our daily affairs, the way we cope.

The view is current, in scientific research and popular educational theorizing, that the brain is an information-processing device, functioning only under the press of immediate circumstances to seek, organize, retrieve, and utilize information. Learning is regarded as the acquisition of information; memory, its recovery; and thinking, its manipulation. This narrow and ugly metaphor, taken directly from contemporary electronic technology, regards the brain as a kind of computer, a device for performing a limited set of predetermined operations on data. But this is not what the brain is, or what it does.[1]

The brain is more like an artist than a machine. It constantly creates realities, actual and imaginary; it examines alternatives, spins stories, and thrives on experience. The brain picks up huge amounts of "information" on our journey through life, but only incidentally, the way our shoes pick up mud when we walk through the woods. Knowledge is a byproduct of experience, and experience is what thinking makes possible.

THE BUSINESS OF THE BRAIN

We are constantly thinking about what the world is like, and what it is likely to be like, and even about worlds that are most unlikely. Our expectations about the world constantly change as a consequence of our experience, and in the process we collect—*construct* might be a better word—"knowledge" or "information." The present would be incomprehensible if we could not relate it to the past, and meaningless if we could not relate it to the future. We are constantly thinking. We think *with* the contents of the brain, not *about* them.

Feelings are always focal in the continual flow of commonplace thinking, as we make sense of the world we are in, avoid bewilderment, achieve satisfaction, escape frustration, and confirm our own identity, our role as author and character in the ongoing story of our life.[2] There is no one way of summing up what the brain does in the course of the day, in the course of our life, not because it does many different things, but because what it does is manifested in so many different ways. Perhaps the poet's insight captures it best: The human brain imposes order on chaos.

We are thinking on those occasions when we would say we were not thinking. If we walk down the street without colliding with other people, we must be thinking. If we collide with other people it is probably because we are thinking about other things; our attention is elsewhere. If we do something "without thinking," we have thought about it differently from the way we subsequently wish we had. The brain never stops thinking.

Absence of awareness of thinking is not absence of thinking. Thought is never conscious. What we "hear" and "see" in our head when we imagine ourselves thinking is a product of thinking rather than thinking itself. Thinking underlies all of the private "in-the-head" phenomena of which we are aware; it underlies what we say when we talk to ourselves as it does when we talk to others.

Lack of awareness of why we have behaved in particular ways certainly does not indicate that no thinking has taken place.[3] Even when we behave habitually, the particular habits that we engage in are initiated by some aspect of thinking. We do not engage in habits at random; they manifest themselves at appropriate times (or at what once would have been appropriate times). Even when a habit might seem totally undesirable in particular circumstances—when we find ourselves doing something we wish we had not started—it has probably been initiated by a course of thinking that we wish we had been able to resist, rather than by an absence of thinking. "I wasn't thinking" is a conventional way of expressing regret about behavior, but not an indication of mental shutdown. Even daydreaming involves thinking, untrammeled by any concern with present circumstances. Oversights occur when we are thinking about something else, not when we are not thinking.

Commonplace thought is complex. We tend to think that we go through the day thinking of just one thing at a time and that it is unusual, disruptive even, to be attending to more than one thing simultaneously. But the brain routinely takes many considerations into account, including balancing contrary plans, purposes, and intentions, in determining the smooth flow of daily life.

We are not guided by just one intention at a time. At any moment a whole range of intentions and considerations determine the way in which we behave. Ask a friend why she is hurrying, and she may say she is late for class. Why is she going to the class? Because it is part of a course she is taking. Why has she selected that course? Because it is part of her degree program. Why is she working on that particular degree? The reasons may include all kinds of practical and career considerations, themselves determined by numerous social and personal factors. If she decides that she is not interested in the course, or if she has conflicting demands on her time that make it difficult for her to get to that particular class, then the alternative decision she will make will take into account all the overriding factors. Everything she does, and every alternative she considers, will still be congruent with a number of concerns. Sometimes, of course, considerations conflict; our friend's career is important to her, but she wants to keep a particular morning free for some other reason.

We rarely do something for just one reason, even if we spend an evening watching television. We can usually relate what we are doing right now to plans we have for the next few minutes, hours, days, months, and years. The rich fabric of our plans and intentions constitutes a specification that we have for our life, including our hopes and expectations from the present to the distant future. We all have some idea of what is likely to be happening to us in the next few minutes, hours, days, months, and years—even if there are alternative possibilities that we cannot decide among.[4]

All this may sound complex and esoteric, but we think in these ways all the time, without realizing what we are doing, when we are driving a car or reading a book. We make decisions about what to do next based on intricate considerations of what we want to do in the future and of what is likely to happen at various times from the immediate present to years ahead. Commonplace thought is full of complex decisions, routinely but efficaciously made.

MAKING DECISIONS

Perception, psychologists like to say, is decision-making. The brain has no direct contact with the outside world; that world is a reality that the brain has to create. Secluded in the dark and silent vault of the skull, the brain has no sensitivity of its own (it feels pain only for the rest of the body) and no direct awareness of its situation in the world. The brain's only connection with the outside world is through arrays of nerve fibers radiating to the eyes, ears, skin, and other "receptor organs." The eyes are not "windows on the world," they send no pictures to the brain—and if they did the brain has no inner eye with which to inspect them. The neural impulses that pass back and forth between the brain and the eyes are a stuttering barrage of bioelectrical energy, no different in quality from the volleys of neural impulses that pass between the brain and the ears or any other part of the body. They are not "messages" from anyone or anything. The brain must *decide* what is initiating those incoming neural assaults; it must *create* the sights, sounds, and other events that we perceive as images of the world. Everything we see, hear, touch, or otherwise perceive, the drama as well as the fabric of life, is something we *think* we have experienced in the world.[5]

We do not see what is in front of our eyes, but what we think is in front of our eyes. Nothing in the world announces itself to us. If I see a horse in front of me, it is because I have decided that it is a horse I am looking at. The more I want to see a horse, or expect to see a horse, the more likely I am to see a horse, even if I am looking at a cow. If I am convinced that the next person to come around the corner will be my friend, then the next person to come around the corner will quite possibly be my friend, at first glance at least. We have all had demonstrations of the power of suggestion—even autosuggestion—to influence what we see and hear. We have only to think of the way our apprehensions rule our perceptions when we are alone at night, in unfamiliar surroundings, or when our nervous expectations have been primed by a macabre book or movie.

The brain can be mistaken in the perceptual decisions that it makes, but most of the time it does not let us down. It is rarely reluctant to make perceptual decisions, and it decides and creates so efficiently that we are seldom aware of all the thinking that is going on every time we see, hear, smell, taste or touch anything that we recognize. All of this involves categorization, classification, and inferences; it is all "high-level" abstract thinking. We would be continually confused, living in a surrealistic dream, if the brain were unable or reluctant to make these continual existential decisions.

The brain also makes endless decisions involving behavior. We decide to get up at a particular time, we decide to dress, and how to dress, and what to have for breakfast (if we decide to have breakfast), and where to go first, and how to get there, and what to do when we arrive. Every step along the way during the day, with scarcely any call on our conscious attention, the brain plans, organizes, anticipates, categorizes, chooses, infers, solves problems, determines relationships, and makes decisions. Life would be a shambles without constant thought of the most complex kind, even among children. It is remarkable that the idea ever got abroad that children cannot think, or that they can lack "essential thinking skills."

Of course, we all make mistakes from time to time. But a wrong or inappropriate conclusion is usually a consequence of not knowing enough in the first place, or of taking false considerations into account, rather than of lacking vital skills. My ability to think collapses when I am confronted by an article on nuclear physics, but not because I need to take courses in logic, problem-solving, or reasoning.

There are also occasions when we cannot make up our mind, just as there are occasions when we wish we had decided differently. But the occasions when we become caught in confusion and error only serve to underline the fact that the brain generally makes superbly efficient decisions.

Sometimes we have difficulty making decisions because we have no particular reason for deciding one way or another, or because the matter we must decide is trivial. We vacillate between scrambled and poached eggs in the morning because the question is hardly worth thinking about, we have more important things on our mind, and little rests on the outcome. But at the other extreme we have difficulty making up our mind when a great deal is at stake and we are unsure of the consequences of the decision. Shall we risk the uncertain opportunities of a new job or retain the security of our present situation? Should we take a vacation, replace the car, or keep our savings intact? Will a course of action we are contemplating make us look incompetent? Will we be able to explain our reasons? If we cannot make these kinds of decision, it is not because we lack essential decision-making skills but because we are apprehensive about the consequences. Sometimes we just do not want the responsibility of making a decision—and sometimes we do not have the authority to do so.

There are no generalizable decision-making skills, for the simple reason that there is no general class of "decisions" to be made. Decisions depend upon circumstances. No all-purpose techniques can be learned to ensure that better decisions will be made. Making better decisions about particular matters or states of affairs requires more experience of those matters or states of affairs. Willingness to make decisions on particular occasions involves personal (and personality) considerations, not cognitive strategies. And where authority to make decisions is restrained politically, the remedy has to be political.

PROBLEM-SOLVING

Our brains are constantly solving problems. Every time we learn, or remember, or make sense of something, we solve a problem. Some psychologists have characterized all infant language-learning as problem-solving, extending to children such scientific procedures as "learning by experiment," or "hypothesis-testing."[6] Grown-ups rarely explain the meaning of new words to children, let alone how grammatical rules work. Instead they use the words or the rules in conversation and leave it to children to figure out what is going on. In order to learn language, an infant must make sense of the contexts in which language occurs; problems must be solved. We have all been solving problems of this kind since childhood, usually without awareness of what we are doing. Confronted by an insoluble problem, we are stymied, baffled, uncertain about what to do next. This happens to everyone at times, of course, but it is not a common state of affairs. It is rare to see adults, or even children, immobilized because they do not know what to do next—except in bureaucratic or educational situations.

The term *problem-solving* is broad and imprecise, even though some people think that generalizable "problem-solving skills" can be taught. But there is no one category of events in the world that can be called problems, the way there are related and recognizable events that might be called sunsets, or football games. What is a problem for me might not be a problem for you. And behavior that solves one problem might not solve another. Some problems are technical, requiring various kinds of technical knowledge and solutions. There are mathematical or chess or word problems, or problems concerning the best way to display data on a graph, install a telephone, cut down a tree, repair a leaky faucet, locate specific information in a library, read a map, find a route from one side of town to the other, or select the right piece of equipment to buy. Other problems are social—discovering why a friend is unhappy or how to work collaboratively with a colleague—and many may be personal, usually related to the way we perceive ourselves or others perceive us.

These different kinds of problem have nothing in common, and no particular kind of strategy could solve them all. Just as there is no general class of problems, so there can be no general class of solutions. Procedures or "strategies"—such as "identify the nature of the problem," "define and clarify essential elements and terms," "judge and connect relevant information," or "list possible alternative solutions"— are too obvious and too vague to be of any practical use. Often the problem cannot be identified until it is solved, or it is solved with the identification. The difficulty with many of the problems we have to solve (as opposed to those we solve without being aware that we have dealt with them) is usually not failure to consider the nature of the problem or to reflect on possible solutions, but inability to find an appropriate way to think about it. We do not know enough about what we are trying to think about. We lack knowledge rather than skills.

The resolution for many problems is an arbitrary decision rather than an irrefutable solution; the problems are dilemmas, we cannot find solutions that are practical, or we dislike every alternative. We do not know which way to turn, we are not prepared to compromise or to pay a price. Often the problem is *other people*: The difficulty is changing *their* behavior. Generalized instruction is not going to make us better at solving any of these problems. We need more experience of the particular kind of issue—or person—we are dealing with, and possibly better understanding of our own propensities and habits.

Nevertheless, we do solve problems, routinely, without effort or awareness. These are like the more conscious problems I have just mentioned, but they have smaller dimensions. They get us through the day, but they do not command our attention. We are not apprehensive about their outcome. We solve "technical" problems—the "word puzzles" of understanding what other people are saying; the "math problems" of making change; the practical problems of looking up a telephone number, pruning a plant, mixing hot and cold water, making purchases, finding the section of the newspaper that we want to read or the route to a place we want to go. We continually solve social problems of how to interact with people we know and people who are strangers, and we solve personal problems of how to present or regard ourselves at particular moments of the day.

I have deliberately selected commonplace examples to parallel the larger-scale kinds of problem I referred to a few paragraphs ago, but a catalog of problems that we routinely face and solve during the day would be endless. Every step along the way throughout the waking day we are solving problems. The difference between the occasional problems that command so much of our attention and the commonplace ones that we cope with all the time is not that they are different kinds of problem, requiring different kinds of skill, but that we are much more concerned with the outcome or we are dealing with something we do not understand. If we cannot solve these problems, it is not because we lack general problem-solving skills.[7]

Solving problems is essentially no different from anything else the brain does. Problem-solving cannot be separated from decision-making, categorizing, classifying, inferring, and other aspects of thinking, often listed as distinct skills. Problem-solving can be seen to involve, and be involved in, all these aspects of thought. They are not distinctive elements but simply ways of looking at, or talking about, one coherent thing, the brain's construction of realities, the imposition of order on chaos.

The variety of terms that refer to aspects of thinking exist for our conceptual convenience only. That is the reason I have separated "decision-making" from "problem-solving" in this chapter and will now go on to discuss "reasoning." But there is nothing about this new topic that is different from anything I have said so far.

REASONING

Reasoning is also not a unique, clearly distinguishable mental activity—or at least, it is not a word with a unique, clearly distinguishable application. Sometimes the word is used synonymously with thinking in general; in fact, "reasoning" is a common definition of *thinking*. Reasoning sometimes involves justifying a conclusion already made; sometimes, persuading another person to accept a conclusion. It can be an explanation of the past or an argument about the future. The only thing all these different aspects of reasoning would seem to have in common is that they involve moving from one state of affairs to another, or accounting for how (or why) such a movement took place. To talk of "chains of reasoning" is not such an inappropriate metaphor; reasoning attempts to tie thoughts or actions together in an unbroken series of links.

But the metaphor should not be used to justify the outmoded and sterile notion that thinking and reasoning are simply a matter of "making associations."[8] Everything the brain does (like everything human beings do) can be regarded as making associations. Everything can be "associated" with everything else in one way or another. What matters is the nature of the associations—whether they are practical, or plausible, or defensible. No general criteria can be presented for what makes a good argument, an acceptable rationale, or appropriate reasoning, because everything depends on the context, on what is being reasoned about. You do not become a good reasoner by learning rules of rhetoric (although there are innumerable conventions about the proper way to reason about particular subjects in particular circumstances). Ability to reason comes with understanding what you are endeavoring to reason about.

There are no general rules that will make anyone an expert reasoner in matters of domestic finances, computer programming, or political theory. What is needed is experience in handling money, programming computers, and engaging in politics.

Besides, there can be no hard-and-fast rules of reasoning, because different people can reason from what might appear to be exactly the same premises and come to quite different conclusions. Politicians of varying persuasions consistently come to quite contrary conclusions, not necessarily because most of them cannot reason, but rather because they use reasoning to support their preconceived points of view. Reasoning is often used to justify a position rather than to achieve the most appropriate one. Reasoning can be used to justify any desired position. When we insist that other people reason fallaciously, we usually mean that we disagree with the conclusions that they reach.

Besides, the links in a chain of reasoning are never complete; there are always missing premises that have to be filled in by the listener (or reader) if the reasoning is to be "followed." No one has the patience, or the knowledge, to specify or examine every consideration upon which an argument is based. If I hear that a child was absent from school because of illness, I am likely to assume (rightly or wrongly) that it was the child who was ill, not another family member, and that the child is currently ill, and that the child is confined to home, if not to bed. But none of these conditions is specified in the original statement; I have supplied them all myself (and quite possibly I was expected to supply them when the actual state of affairs happened to be quite different). Missing premises are "presuppositions"; they are "understood" in the sense that they literally go without saying—speakers expect this contribution from listeners to avoid unnecessary and interminable explanations, and listeners expect to make this contribution to avoid the boredom of listening to speakers saying things they already know. But the links could never be complete, no matter how hard one tries. Some things must always remain unsaid; otherwise statements would never end.

Some logicians refer to this filling in of missing premises as "charity" (Johnson & Blair, 1985)—listeners help to complete arguments for speakers. But as Johnson and Blair point out, charity begins at home—

we tend to interpret arguments in the way that is most plausible to ourselves.

However reasoning is defined, it is not an exotic or uncommon activity. It is something else the brain does all the time—or rather, a continual part of what the brain does all the time. We do not usually behave unthinkingly. When we do things, we do them for a reason (even if they sometimes turn out to be unfortunate things for undesirable reasons). We may occasionally behave recklessly, but rarely randomly. If I go to a store, it is because I have reasons for going to the store. If I buy a book, it is because I have reasons for buying a book. I also have reasons if I decline to buy a book. The brain reasons effortlessly and unobtrusively. As with decision-making and problem-solving, we only become aware of reasoning (and of supposed inadequacies in reasoning) when we run into difficulty, in particular when we try to reason about something we do not know a great deal about (which may sometimes include our own motivation for behaving in particular ways or believing particular things). But no "skills" of reasoning will make us think better in these situations, though more experience, or a different attitude, might make a difference.

When we say that other people do not reason, we mean that they come to different conclusions from our own, or that they cannot give reasons for coming to a particular decision—or reasons that satisfy our own reasoning. People who do not reason the way we think they should don't think the way we think they should. The way we reason is not the way people in other cultures reason—not because we have different levels of skill, but because we have different worldviews. Culture is the way we rationalize the world.

Our own reasoning is frequently *post hoc*; we do or decide something and then reason why we did or decided it. We do not act or think out of character—our constantly thinking brain always shapes our behavior in characteristic ways, including the characteristic ways in which we jump to conclusions. And it usually is not difficult to find a convenient rationale for our reasoning about why we did what we did. If we wanted to—and could see things from the other person's point of view—we could find other people's rationale for thinking the way they do.

FORMAL AND INFORMAL LOGIC

It is widely believed that many people are incapable of thinking logically, and that as a consequence the quality of their thinking suffers. Both beliefs are false. Everyone—even children—can think logically, if they can think at all. But logic, of the formal textbook kind, is not a particularly good way to think; it can lead to problems. We all have a better way of thinking, more natural than logic.

The crucial limitation of formal logic is that it is mechanical, literally thought-less. Logic only guarantees that a conclusion is *valid*, that it follows inexorably from its premises. It cannot guarantee that a conclusion is correct (it may be based on false premises) or that it is desirable (there may be better alternatives). Logic functions like a computer program. Computers do exactly what their programming requires them to do, even if consequences are absurd. "Garbage in, garbage out" applies to logic as well as to computer programming.

Computers think logically, which is the reason their thinking can never be trusted. They do not have values or common sense (and if values and common sense are programmed into them, computers are incapable of interpreting values and common sense in value-based and commonsense ways). Committees and bureaucrats tend to think logically, which is the reason they can on occasion come to absurd conclusions. They reach conclusions that are valid according to the rules, or according to the given premises, but that make no sense in terms of human desirability or values.

Values and common sense are what humans have that is better than logic, and humans use their values and common sense to override logic. This is the way our brains work. If we reach a conclusion that we think undesirable, then we change the premises (we may actually believe we heard or read something different) or we manufacture a more acceptable conclusion.

The research literature is replete with documentation of adults and children in many cultures misunderstanding arguments or fabricating chains of reasoning in order to come to conclusions consistent with their own values and ideas of common sense. Perhaps the best examples are provided by the investigations of the Russian psychologist Luria (1976) into the thought of illiterate (but not ignorant) Russian peasants. He presented them with logical arguments in classical syllogistic form, such as *In the Far North . . . all bears are white. Novaya Zemlya is in the Far North. . . . What color are the bears there?* The "illogical" replies included "I don't know. I've seen a black bear, I've never seen any others"; "There are different kinds of bears"; "I've never seen one, and hence I can't say"; and even "Your words can only be answered by someone who was there, and if a person wasn't there he can't say anything on the basis of your words." Obviously, the peasants did not know how to participate in the game the experimenter was playing (or did not want to). But was this for lack of essential thinking skills?

What interferes with logical reasoning, in other words, is *sense*. We reach conclusions that other people might dispute not because we fail to exercise logic but because we have different points of view. The persistence of so many profound religious, political, and scientific controversies, even among people of impeccable intellectual qualifications and manifest goodwill, is clear evidence that logic cannot be the ruling principle underlying the decisions and conclusions we make about the world. We are governed by our values and our common sense—both a consequence of our experience. When there is disagreement, it is usually not because individuals cannot think logically but because their values and common sense conflict with other people's.

Formal logic has become so discredited as a model for actual or ideal ways for individuals to think (among some theorists at least) that an entirely different area of study has been developed focusing on "informal logic." Unfortunately, and for the kinds of considerations I have already mentioned, some people are now assuming that individuals are incapable of informal logical thought unless they receive special kinds of instruction. But informal logic is the way people naturally think.[9]

"HIGHER-ORDER THINKING"

Unlike most of the "thinking" words and terms with which we have so far been concerned, *higher-order thinking* is not in common use. It does not crop up in daily conversation. It is not to be found in standard dictionaries. The term occurs most frequently in psychological and educational parlance, but not because it is especially clear or conceptually useful. On the contrary, people who use the term most may spend a good deal of time asking what higher-order thinking is. They look for definitions. They assume that there are not only different kinds of thinking but also different levels of thinking (and different levels of thinkers). The general point of view seems to be that higher-order thinking is not only the most efficient but also the most difficult kind of thinking. Not everyone can do it, but all the best thinkers can.

In other words, *higher-order thinking* is a status term. Like all status terms, it discriminates. And like many forms of discrimination, it is based on purely imaginary distinctions. The term discriminates first of all among presumed different ways of thinking. It implies that some kinds of thinking are low-grade, low-quality, inferior imitations or substitutes for the "real thing." No researcher has distinguished higher-order and lower-order thinking in any kind of brain or behavior study, but because of the emphasis on the need to teach higher-order thinking, the assumption is that low-grade thinking is the natural and possibly preferred state of the brain—habitual, careless, "sloppy," and untutored.

Higher-order thinking, by contrast, is presumed to be a superior mix of high-value attributes or components, such as planning, predicting, monitoring, evaluating, and questioning, together with some impressive couplets of procedures, such as analysis and synthesis, and induction and deduction. Higher-order thinking often includes an "executive" function that is able to take charge and exercise leadership, at least in its own affairs. Higher-order thinking is presumed to be more complex, more recondite, requiring more attention and a superior brain.[10]

This leads to the second way in which the notion of higher-order thinking discriminates among people. Not everyone is supposed to be capable of reaching elevated levels of thought, certainly not without great effort and painstaking instruction. The people who are natural and accomplished higher-order thinkers are preeminently academic—professors, or students who do well at academic subjects, the earners of the high grades—together with other high-status successes and leaders in predominant cultures. "Underprivileged" populations are not expected to produce higher-order thinkers.

But all the supposed elements of higher-order thinking are in fact commonplace. They are not separate activities at all, but a continuous and intrinsic part of everyday thought—and they are not done badly. They only look difficult when pulled out of everyday contexts and made the topic of special forms of instruction and tests, where the critical feature is often an understanding of the language and of the expectations of the designers of the instructional materials and tests.

We are planning and predicting every moment of our lives—what we will be doing in the next few moments, the next few hours, the next few days. We all monitor and evaluate, perhaps more than we should, the consequences of our own thinking and the thinking of other people.

Everybody questions, even the youngest infant.[11] The brain is not doing anything different when it questions, although we talk differently when we put questions into words. There is no skill of *questioning*, although it is necessary to know how to ask questions (the appropriate language to put them in) and when to ask them (another conventional matter). It is also necessary to know what kinds of question to ask in particular circumstances—but that knowledge comes with a general understanding of the circumstances. There is no way I can ask intelligent questions about nuclear physics, not because I lack essential questioning skills, but because of my ignorance of nuclear physics.

Other putative higher-order thinking skills sound even more esoteric in the abstract, such as setting deadlines, establishing priorities, identifying and allocating resources, and knowing when to stop thinking about something. But once again, we are all consistently very good at such "management strategies" in everyday life, provided we are engaged in (or thinking about) an activity that we are familiar with and not plagued by apprehension or uncertainty. If we think impulsively or compulsively, it is for personality or experiential reasons, not because we have faulty thinking abilities.

Analyzing and *synthesizing* are specialist terms for particular characteristics of reasoning that are commonplace and inseparable. The distinction is a conceptual one and exists only on paper. No one thinks purely analytically, or purely synthetically—in fact, it is impossible to do one without the other. What is called "analytic thought" is thought that focuses on detail, on parts rather than the whole, that is perhaps particularly persistent and critical; but it is not a different kind of thinking. What is called "synthetic thinking" is supposed to bring elements together. But the details we perceive are always related to a larger picture, parts to a whole. The world cannot be perceived in fragments; every figure needs a ground in order to be distinguished.

It is impossible to engage in analytic and synthetic thought without engaging in both induction and deduction, which are also often assumed to be separate and distinctive components of higher-order thought. But everyone constantly engages in thought that is both inductive and deductive, and it is impossible to do one without the other, or without doing anything else. Perception, in the constructive manner I have discussed, is deductive, moving from "generals" (what is known or assumed) to "particulars" (what is actually seen or heard). Learning, in the sense of creating general laws or expectations from the observation of specific instances, could be characterized as inductive. But perception never takes place in the absence of learning or learning without perception.

It is difficult to distinguish deduction from what in other circumstances is called *problem-solving*. And concept learning, inference, and reasoning by analogy are all instances of inductive reasoning. (Detectives typically induce, rather than deduce.) None of these things can be done separately from each other, or from anything else. They are pseudocategories.

It will be helpful to remind ourselves why all these different "thinking" terms have come into the language. It is not because they have been found necessary to label recognizably different mental processes. Instead, they refer to different circumstances, or states of affairs, and in those contexts they make complete sense. Some of the words are only used by specialists (like logicians with *induction* and *deduction*), but in these cases the specialists know what the words refer to—and they are not referring to brain processes. When words are employed in familiar contexts, no one has to ask what the words mean. They relate to what an individual is obviously doing on a particular occasion, not what the individual's brain is imagined to be doing. Our language would be drab and uninformative indeed if we simply used the word *think* all the time, but only because we would have to use many other qualifying words to describe particular situations.

Nevertheless, the psychological theorists who speculate about the private internal operations of the brain often find it necessary to devise new terms and distinctions for the complex multilevel architectures that they construct. A popular contemporary distinction is between *cognitive* and *metacognitive* reasoning. Metacognitive thought is thought that is above or beyond normal cognition, since its object is cognition itself.[12]

Monitoring, reviewing, reflecting, and revising are regarded as "metacognitive" skills, involving thinking about thinking, which is regarded as a higher kind of thinking than thinking about anything else. "Observing" and "controlling" one's own thought processes are supposed to be different and superior modes of thinking, not practiced by many people because they have not learned how. But once again these are all fictitious and prejudicial concepts, favored by people with vested interests in finding ways of categorizing individuals—usually schoolchildren—in discriminatory ways. No one needs to learn *how* to think about the consequences of their own thought, although we all have differing propensities to become analytical (and self-critical) in particular circumstances.

Besides, we cannot observe our own thought processes. We are not aware of them, and they cannot be inspected in oneself or in anyone else. They are obscured in a world of neurological and chemical flux which no one can read or translate. What we are aware of when we listen to the inner voice of introspection is a *product* of our own thought— and no one is deaf to that voice.

How could "thinking about thinking" be different from thinking about anything else? We usually know when we do not understand something, or when we have solved a problem, at least to our own satisfaction. If we do not know these things on a particular occasion, it is not because we lack certain skills; we just do not understand sufficiently what we are trying to do (or we are not paying enough attention, which is a matter of our disposition in particular circumstances rather than lack of a special skill).

EASY AND DIFFICULT THINKING

As I have been emphasizing, thinking is usually easy, a common-place affair. We think all the time, without effort, without awareness, and usually without gross error. We become aware of thinking only when it becomes difficult, when it would be appropriate to think differently from the way we are thinking at the moment, or when our current thinking leads us into unpleasant or undesirable situations.

Thinking is easy and effective when two fundamental requirements are met. The first I have already discussed: the need to understand what we are thinking about. If we are in a situation that we do not understand, thinking is bound to be difficult and confused. The problem is not that we cannot think but that we have nothing solid to think about. Precisely the same consideration applies to language. No matter how articulate we are, we have difficulty talking if we do not understand what we are trying to talk about. The observation should be too trite to be made, except for the fact that in some educational situations, students who do not understand what they are supposed to be thinking and talking or writing about are classified as being deficient in thinking or language skills.

The second requirement for easy and effective thinking I have not discussed directly, although it is implicit in much of what has been said in this chapter. Thinking is easy and effective when the brain itself is in charge, in control of its own affairs, going about its own business.

What it means exactly to say that the brain must be in control of its own affairs will be examined at some length later in this book, when the overall, ongoing operation of the brain is considered. For the present, the condition may be best explained by considering the alternative: Thinking becomes difficult and inefficient when the brain loses control, when what we try to think about is *contrived* rather than an integral part of whatever we would otherwise be engaged in at the moment. Thinking is difficult when we stop whatever we would otherwise be doing in order to concentrate on thinking about a particular topic, or problem, or passage in a book. Contrived thinking of this kind goes against the predominant tendency of thought; in effect it throws the brain out of gear. Something that in less forced circumstances might be thought about with ease becomes an obstacle, a blurred focus of contrary purposes, aggravated often by frustration and irritation. The brain is no longer in charge. And the most difficult kind of thinking is that which is imposed on us by someone else, when our own brain can be totally disconnected from what we are expected to be thinking about.

The need for the brain to be in control of its own thinking is obviously related to the first requirement—that we must understand what we are thinking about. An inevitable consequence of much contrived thinking—whether the contrivance is by ourselves or by other people—is that the brain no longer understands what it is doing. But now the reason for the lack of understanding may not be ignorance, but simply the fact that the brain is not in tune with what it is supposed to be thinking about; it is basically trying to think of something else.

Another way of looking at these matters is to consider the purposes of particular episodes of thought. When thinking is done for ourselves, in the course of getting us through our daily affairs, or pursuing particular flights of fancy or personal interest, then we have no trouble with it. We are not even aware that thinking is taking place. That is the reason that we do not give ourselves and other people credit for all the highly efficient thinking that is such a commonplace achievement—it is done so well and effortlessly that we do not realize that we are thinking. Paradoxically, it is only difficult and inefficient thinking that we become aware of, in ourselves and in others, and as a consequence it is widely believed that most thinking is difficult and inefficient.

When thinking is done at the behest of other people, on the other hand, or when it is done with other people in mind—in order to participate in a conversation, for example, or in some kind of public forum—then it becomes contrived and difficult. I want to draw a distinction that is rarely made between *private* and *social* thinking, not in the sense that these are different kinds of thinking, which they are not, but in the sense that they are thinking done in different circumstances, for different reasons. The degree of control exercised by the brain is different.

Private and Social Thinking

Thinking done for totally personal reasons—even when it concerns other people—usually has secure roots in our own intentions, values, considerations, and desires. We usually know where we are coming from and where we want to get to, and our thoughts can range without the inhibition of other people's possible reaction. The business of the brain is the construction of realities—the actual present reality of the world in which we live and the alternative realities of possible (and impossible) worlds that exist, at the moment, only in our own mind.

There is much fantasy in private thought, but not necessarily of the escapist kind. Wishful thinking about the future may constitute detailed planning or rehearsal for coming possibilities. Rueful thinking, when we reconstruct the past the way we wish it had been, can often be preparation for similar circumstances in the future. Both wishful and rueful thinking can be experiences from which we learn, even if the experiences transpire entirely in our own head. Talking to oneself can be particularly productive in a world where "communication skills" are so important. Whether we imagine the interview or conversation we hope to have in the future, or recapitulate or revise a discussion we had in the past, it is all experience from which we can profit.

Personal thinking can, of course, be highly idiosyncratic; it is self-oriented, inquisitive, and expressive. But it is what gets us through life in our own way. Social thinking (or, rather, the way we think in order to interact with other people) tends to be more consensual, other-oriented. It has more constraints. Teachers, colleagues, officials, family members, and friends influence how we think and what we think about. They evaluate the consequences of our thought, distracting its course. We may not think we are making a mistake, but other people may. Other people may not think their thinking is defective, but we do. In other words, thinking about how people think frequently involves value judgments that are absent from personal commonplace thinking.

Of course, we all make mistakes. But we are also sensitive to mistakes, to consequences of thought that were not intended. When we are unaware of thinking mistakes, it is usually because we would not recognize them as errors if they were pointed out to us. The problem with a good deal of thinking is where it starts from, not the course it takes. We can have strange ideas in our head. It is not that we do not know enough, but that we know, or believe, inaccurate or inappropriate things. Next to persuading people to change their mind, the hardest thing to do is to persuade them that not everyone sees the world the way they do, or that those who have a different point of view are not necessarily wrong.

Questioning our own beliefs is difficult, but not because we do not have the skills to do it. Children change their mind all the time as they learn about the world. But as we grow older we develop an investment in the way we see the world (which is indistinguishable from the way we see ourselves), and trying to get people to change their worldview challenges the carefully built-up feelings they have of their own identity. One of the major functions of thinking is to create an identity for ourselves, with a supportive rationale.

Personal Factors

Finally, there is the matter of habitual attitudes, dispositions, and propensities, none of which can be taught, and possibly not even trained, except through example, facilitation, and support. I am referring to such personal characteristics as reflectiveness (or impulsiveness), attention span, concentration (narrow focus), contemplation (broad focus), tolerance of uncertainty and ambiguity, patience with other people, and willingness to face facts, to change one's mind, and to admit one is wrong.

But as I make this list I recognize that none of the items is a general characteristic that some people have and others lack. There are some things that I am quite reflective about, that I will dwell upon for quite a long while, but others I just cannot be bothered with. I am willing to change my mind about some things, but not about others. Even matters of relative energy and self-esteem are dependent on particular activities and subjects rather than on general personality traits applicable to a person as a whole. Even lethargic people seem capable of summoning remarkable effort and determination about some things. To regard matters of attention, effort, and direction as "mental discipline" or "correct habits," which can be taught or acquired, misses the point.

Thinking for ourselves is the way we normally think—and it is a way of thinking that is concealed from ourselves and from others because it is commonplace, usually effective, and effortless. Thinking at the behest of others is difficult. Not only is our brain thrown out of gear, but we must often provide explanations about something we did not reflect upon in the first place; we are expected to map out a route to a particular decision or action when we were never conscious of the path we were following. In some educational contexts we must learn the specialized metacognitive language for talking about thinking. Sharing reflections on our own thought is less a matter of looking into our own heads (which is impossible) than of knowing the language to use for the occasion.

We talk differently about thinking to different people—and must adjust our thinking accordingly. Compare the assertive way in which teachers describe their "thinking" to children (when the teachers may be reciting an explanation they have themselves learned) with the tentative manner in which children explain their thinking to teachers. There are similar differences in the way employers and employees explain themselves to each other, or individuals at the various levels of bureaucratic hierarchies. And people who are required to talk differently are unlikely to think alike.

To summarize, thinking is not an occasional mental activity; it goes on all the time, without awareness. Thinking organizes reality for us, and our own place in those realities, and creates alternative realities that we might hope to achieve (or to avoid).

Thinking is not a set of acquired skills, but rather a matter of experience, of understanding the requirements and conventions of particular subject matters. Not everyone will be a fast or effective thinker—there are natural differences, just as there are differences in how fast individuals can run. But everyone free of gross and evident physiological impairment thinks, and thinks competently. Usually when we think badly it is due to our own particular experience, values, or dispositions, rather than to a lack of anything essential in our ability to think.

Thinking is also not an exclusive activity, something that we can do separately from anything else. We do not suspend learning, remembering, or other aspects of mental life in order to engage in thought. Rather, thought permeates everything we do—it is the business of the brain. The intimate relationship of thinking to other aspects of mental life—which the brain also normally accomplishes effortlessly and remarkably well—is the subject to which we turn in the following chapter.

3

REMEMBERING, UNDERSTANDING, AND LEARNING

A universal characteristic of language is that speakers need not say what listeners can be expected to know. If I remark that I used a credit card to pay a restaurant bill, I need not add that it was because I had eaten a meal there. The meal can be taken for granted, or "presupposed," as linguists say. I would only mention a meal if for some reason I had not eaten one, or if there had been something unusual about it. When we read about a marathon, we do not expect to be told that the runners were all wearing clothes, though we would be told if they were not.

"Thinking" is rarely remarked upon in everyday conversation, not because little thinking is done in the course of the day, but because thinking can be presupposed. There are more specific words for all the activities we engage in that involve thinking, and we use those words instead. Thinking is not mentioned unless it requires a particular effort or if it might look as if we were doing nothing. It would be odd to say that we are writing and thinking, or reading and thinking, not because reading and writing do not involve thinking, but because the thinking can be presupposed. We would normally only say we were thinking if we were seated at a desk, *not* engaging in some obvious activity, and afraid of giving the impression that we were asleep.

In education, however, reading and writing are not always assumed to presuppose thinking. Nor are remembering, understanding (or comprehension), and learning. These behaviors are often discussed as if they are quite different from thinking, mutually exclusive, to be studied in different contexts and taught separately. Thinking is regarded as a different subject matter, even a different set of skills, from remembering, comprehension, and learning.

There is an alternative point of view. The reason people do not normally talk about remembering and thinking (or understanding and thinking, or learning and thinking) is that remembering, understanding, and learning all involve thinking—they are aspects of thinking. In fact, remembering, understanding, and learning can be regarded as byproducts of thinking; we remember, understand, and learn all the time, quite inconspicuously, as we think.

The first stage in demonstrating this close relationship between thought and everything else is to show that remembering, understanding, and learning are not in themselves occasional and distinctive behaviors. Like thinking, remembering, understanding, and learning are commonplace occurrences, continually demonstrated by the brain, and accomplished very effectively indeed.

REMEMBERING

The brain is continuously remembering, without effort or conscious awareness. With rare and frustrating exceptions (unless we are suffering from a serious memory disorder), we remember, with remarkable precision, exactly what we need to remember, when we need to remember it. When we wake in the morning we remember who we are and where we are. We remember what we have planned for the day, and we remember to have breakfast (if we usually have breakfast). We remember to dress before we leave home. We remember the names of our friends, how they look, and possibly their telephone numbers as well. We remember where we work, what time to begin work, and what we should be doing at work.

We do not remember *everything* all the time; we would be totally confused if everything we are capable of remembering came into our minds at once. We remember what we need to remember, on cue. Out of the enormous number of things we could remember about language, for example, we manage to remember just those things that are relevant when we listen to someone talking, or when we read. Right now you are remembering relevant things about language—and about remembering—in order to make sense of what you are reading. It would be dangerous for us to go out into the world alone if our brain was not capable of the most complex remembering feats, without effort or conscious attention, every moment of the day.

Of course, memory lets us down sometimes. We cannot always remember what we *want* to remember. We forget the name of an acquaintance when we would like to remember it; we forget where we left the car keys; we cannot remember the spellings of many words; we forget to stop off at the store to pick up the groceries we wanted. But these exceptions are not necessarily a failure of memory. We remember that we cannot remember names, and become confused. We remember all the places we might have left the car keys, and these obscure the particular place. We remember the correct spelling of troublesome words but we also remember incorrect spellings as well, and we have not learned to distinguish the two (and we cannot forget the incorrect alternatives that we always remember). We are distracted from remembering to go to the store by something more interesting that we remember.

In general we remember all the time, without difficulty, when remembering is part of the flow of events in which we are involved, when we can make sense of what we are doing. Remembering is easy, in other words, when it is not a particular focus of attention, when it is something that happens to us in the course of doing something else. We remember best when we are engaged in an activity that is interesting and meaningful to us, when the brain is in charge of its own affairs—an expression, you will remember, that will be discussed in more detail in due course.

Remembering is difficult when it becomes a deliberate activity, the focus of attention, undertaken against the flow of events. Remembering is difficult when it is *contrived*, when we decide what we want to remember, and when and how we shall remember it. We can make remembering difficult for ourselves. But remembering is especially difficult when someone else decides what has to be remembered and when and how remembering should take place. Then the brain is likely to have no control at all, and remembering becomes very difficult indeed.

We belittle the efficiency of our own memory by paying so much attention to occasional but obvious failures and so little attention to continual but inconspicuous successes. This undervaluing has not been helped by the artificial way memory is usually studied and tested, in the research laboratory and in the classroom. Because of the demands for experimental control in psychological investigations, "remembering" is usually tested hours, days, or weeks after subjects have studied lists of nonsense syllables, or meaningless lists of unrelated words. When asked how much experimental material they can recall, the subjects typically can only respond with very little—and they are told that they have not remembered very much. The fact that the subjects remembered when to come back, and where to come back to, and what the room and the experimenter were like, and what they were to be paid for engaging in such an enterprise, is ignored. Students are often in similar situations, their memory faulted when the only thing they cannot remember about a lesson is the contrived material demanded by the teacher.

Remembering and Thinking

Remembering cannot be separated from thinking. I do not have to stop thinking in order to remember. Remembering is simply thinking about the past. I remember what happened yesterday when I think about yesterday, and I remember that President Kennedy was shot when I think about President Kennedy. And I do not forget about the past when I think about the present. How could I make sense of the present without thinking about the past? I cannot even recognize a familiar face without remembering what that face looks like. The present is inseparable from the past.

Remembering is indistinguishable from thinking. Whenever we think about the past, we remember. Whenever we project our thoughts into the future, we bring thoughts about the past with us. Remembering is simply the past tense of thinking.[1]

UNDERSTANDING

A second continual and commonplace characteristic of the brain is understanding (or *comprehension*, which is the term psychologists and educational researchers employ when they want to make the everyday phenomenon of understanding into a special set of skills; the two terms are as synonymous as any two words can be—the dictionary defines understanding as comprehension and comprehension as understanding).

Understanding is not an unusual condition for anyone to be in. It is the opposite of confusion, and most of the time we are not confused. If we can make sense of our situation in the world right now, if we are not perplexed or bewildered, then we must be in a state of understanding. Outside of educational contexts, confusion is a rare condition for anyone to be in. Most of the time we seem able to make sense of what is going on in the world around us, exactly when we most need to make sense of the world. Infants seem remarkably competent at making sense of the world; they rarely look bewildered.

We wake in the morning and we are not confused. We set out to do what we planned to do without confusion, and we read the morning paper or listen to the morning news without confusion (although we may be perplexed by the motivation of some of the people in the news). There is no need to continue the litany. Understanding is something that everyone is capable of, that everyone demonstrates, in most situations and most of the time, without special exercises or instruction.

Understanding is not a passive activity. We do not wait for things to make sense to us. Understanding, meaningfulness, has to be *imposed* on the world because nothing that takes place in the world is self-explanatory, nothing announces itself. If I understand that the object I am looking at is a chair, that is because I have decided it is a chair. If I could not decide what it was, I would not understand what it was. Yet understanding is not simply a matter of knowing things. We understand what we read in the daily newspaper (most of the time), but not because we know what is in the newspaper. If we read what we already know, we are bored—and I mentioned earlier the linguistic convention that a writer should not tell readers what they might be expected to know. Speakers have the same obligation to listeners. We bring understanding to new events that we read or hear about the way we bring understanding to new situations in the world, by the way in which we are able to construct possible realities. Understanding takes us beyond the known to the new; it makes experience possible.

Of course, understanding also fails us occasionally. We find ourselves in situations in which we can make no sense of what is going on, where someone's behavior or statements bewilder us, where we cannot make a decision because we are confused. But inability to comprehend on these occasions is unlikely to be because we lack requisite skills about how to respond. Taking a course in logical thinking will not help. Failure to understand is much more likely to be a case of inadequate experience. We just do not know enough about what we are trying to understand.

For many people, statistics, or bridge, or computer programming may be a constant conundrum. We all have intellectual "disabilities" that are constant sources of confusion, impenetrable to our comprehension, no matter how hard we try to make sense of them. But none of the roadblocks to understanding will be removed if we take courses in "comprehension skills."

We understand all the time, without difficulty, as part of the flow of events in which we are involved, when we can make sense of what we are doing—when our own brain is in control. Understanding is as natural and continuous as breathing, and like breathing it usually only comes to our attention when we experience difficulty trying to do it. Like remembering, understanding is easy when it is not a particular focus of attention, when we are engaged in something that is interesting, meaningful, and natural to us, when the brain is in charge of its own affairs, pursuing its own purposes jn the light of its own experience. Also like remembering, understanding is difficult in contrived circumstances, when we take it into our heads that we are going to understand a particular movie, novel—or textbook—that is disconnected from our immediate interests and our experience. Experimental psychologists have not studied understanding as much as they have studied remembering or learning, but when they have, it has tended once again to be in contrived and basically nonsensical situations. Experimental subjects are asked to examine arbitrary puzzles or problems, and if they fail—if their past experience is no help to them—they are considered to lack comprehension skills.

The situation is not much different in education. If you study something that you cannot relate to what you know already, that you cannot make sense of and have no interest in, then you are bound to have comprehension difficulties. The number of students diagnosed as having comprehension problems could be an indication of the extent to which schools fail to relate to the experience of students, rather than to any intellectual lack on the students' part.

Understanding and Thinking

It is not possible to separate understanding from thinking as mental processes. The brain is not doing different things when we understand and when we think. Understanding *is* thinking. I do not understand something and then think about it—I cannot understand it without thinking about it. And I cannot think about something and then understand it. My understanding may change in the course of my thinking, but there must be an original understanding that is modified as my thinking continues. Thinking proceeds from understanding to understanding. Understanding, in other words, is simply the present tense of thinking. If we look at how thinking relates to the present, we call it *understanding*, just as thinking is called *remembering* from the perspective of the past.

LEARNING

No one has ever tried to catalog how much individuals learn in a lifetime, or even in a single day. No one would know how to begin. The learning that we do is vast—and almost totally unsuspected.

Commonplace examples illustrate the continual nature of learning.

Ask your friends what they saw on television last night, or at the movies last week, and they can tell you in great detail. They can recall characters, costumes, situations, dialog, and jokes. They can tell you what they had for dinner last Sunday, where they had it, and what they were wearing. If they are interested in sports they can recount the latest sports stories and scores—and other stories and scores possibly going back many years. If they are interested in politics—or business, or the arts, or their neighbors—they can recapitulate entire histories of developments, gossip, and scandals. The events of the day, significant or trivial, stick in our minds the way burrs cling to our clothing. This is all *learning*—commonplace, continual, effortless, and inconspicuous. Everything we can remember we must have learned.

Learning is not difficult. It does not even require deliberate motivation. Most of the time we learn without knowing that we are learning. It is an odd educational idea that learning is sporadic, difficult, and effortful, requiring special motivation, incentives, and rewards. It is an odd educational idea based on meaningless learning.

Learning is so natural that we are uncomfortable and restless any time that we are unable to do it. The moment we find ourselves in a situation where we are learning nothing, we are bored (including, most noticeably, those situations in which we are *trying* to learn). Boredom means we know so much about what is going on, or understand so little of it, that there is nothing to be learned. And boredom is aversive. We no more need to be taught or motivated to avoid boredom and pursue learning than we need to be taught or motivated to avoid suffocation and pursue breathing. Learning, like breathing, is a natural and necessary function of the living person, and we are immediately distressed when the possibility of exercising the function is taken from us.

The amount that children learn about language, especially in their earliest years, is phenomenal. By the age of 4, children are adding twenty words a day to their vocabulary, which already comprises 8,000 words or more. (They do not all know the same 8,000 words, of course; they learn the words their families and friends use.) By the age of 7, children are probably learning an average of twenty-seven words a day, every day of the year, Saturdays, Sundays, and school holidays included. They may have trouble learning the words their teachers put on the wordlists to be studied in class, but they learn without strain the words they hear—or see—being used in relevant and meaningful contexts around them. They learn these words without anyone suspecting that they are learning. Even high school students, with all the distractions they have in their lives, have been estimated to be adding about 3,000 words a year to their vocabulary—as many as 8,000, if they read a lot.[2]

And all of this is learned without the benefit of drills, exercises, and tests. Drills, exercises, and tests interfere with learning of this kind.

It is not only vocabulary that children learn with such facility. They learn grammar, too, and idiom, and many other complex verbal and nonverbal conventions of their language. They do not learn the grammar and idiom of their teachers—unless they see themselves as being like their teachers. They learn the grammar and idiom of their friends, of the kind of people they see themselves as being. No children lack grammar, though they may learn different grammars from the one they are expected to learn.

The vastness of language is still only a small part of the learning we all accomplish in the course of our daily lives, without effort on the part of ourselves or anyone else. We can recognize untold numbers of objects—faces, places, knives, forks, tables, chairs, horses, cows, birds, and trees. Even if we cannot differentiate particular species of birds and trees, we do not confuse them with each other, or with different categories of things. We know how knives and forks are related to tables and chairs, how birds fly and fish swim, where both are to be found, and their relationships to everything else in the world. It is not enough to know what something *is*, a name for it, or a way of recognizing it in the future. We learn what everything has to do with everything else, and we learn to relate language with all of this. All of the complexity we can perceive in the world, or can talk about, is a reflection of the complexity we have in our own head.

We learn so that we conform to the identity we construct for ourselves. Language defines the way we see ourselves as being, and children learn to talk exactly like the kind of person they see themselves as being. Quite unwittingly, without practice or effort, they learn to speak precisely the way their friends talk, and just as unwittingly and inevitably they resist any kind of learning that would result in their being mistaken for any kind of person they do not see themselves as being. *Teaching* children to speak differently is a complete waste of time. They will no more talk the way adults would prefer them to talk than they will wear clothes to match the preferences of anyone but their friends. What we learn is how we see ourselves—and how other people persuade us to see ourselves—not only in the way we talk, but in the way we dress, groom, and ornament ourselves, in the way we organize the world, in our beliefs and attitudes. Every child learns a culture, which is the way we all define ourselves.

Such learning persists far beyond childhood. Adults may struggle without success with textbooks and formal instruction to learn another language. But if they can visit a country where that language is spoken and manage to *see* themselves as inhabitants of that country, immersing themselves in local activities and customs, then not only will they learn to talk as the inhabitants talk, they will eat, drink, dress, and think the way the inhabitants do, without knowing or even willing what is happening. We learn and remember to be like the kind of person we see ourselves as being, without effort.

Easy and Difficult Learning

If learning is normally so easy, why should it sometimes be so difficult? Learning is easy when it is part of the flow of events in which we are involved, when we can make sense of what we are doing, when the brain is in charge of its own affairs. Just like remembering and understanding, learning is easy when it is not a particular focus of attention, when it happens to us in the course of doing something else. We learn best when we are engaged in an activity that is interesting and meaningful to us, where our past experience is relevant.

On the other hand, learning is difficult when it is a deliberate intention, undertaken against the flow of events and made the specific focus of attention. Learning can be difficult when it is oriented to some future goal rather than to present interest. Rote learning is difficult (and only a short-term expedient, because forgetting almost immediately follows). Like remembering and understanding, learning is difficult when it is contrived. We can always make learning difficult for ourselves, but it is especially difficult when someone else decides what we should learn, and when and how the learning will take place. Then the brain is likely to be thrown completely out of gear. Learning that is driven by determination and effort is paradoxically likely to be the least efficient learning of all.

Learning and Experimental Psychology

Ironically, it is contrived learning that has been studied most by experimental psychologists. Contrived learning is the basis of psychology's "laws of learning" that have most influenced education. It has often been seen as the only kind of learning. The reason for experimental psychology's emphasis on contrived learning has been well documented historically. Early psychologists, in the last third of the nineteenth century, wanted to establish their discipline as a science by conducting replicable experiments in laboratories. Learning did not appear to be amenable to experimental control because it was difficult to define a unit of learning that could be measured or counted. And the rate at which individuals learned depended on what they were learning and the degree to which it engaged their interest and past experience. The experimental problem was solved in the 1870s by Herman Ebbinghaus, who inaugurated the study of nonsense as the means of studying learning. "Nonsense syllables"—such as TAV, ROP, and ZEG—constituted "units of learning" that would be uncontaminated by anyone's interest or past experience. Subjects given lists of nonsense syllables (or nonsense shapes or nonsense sounds) to learn always performed in a consistent and predictable manner: The amount of learning that would take place was a direct function of the number of items to be learned and the amount of time or number of trials allowed for practice. Learning was most rapid on the first few items but progressively slowed as the number of items to be learned increased. It was as much as most people could do to learn more than a dozen items on a list, but learning those dozen items was guaranteed—if enough time was spent on the task. Thousands of "learning studies" of this nature have been conducted since, on humans and on animals. (Animal learning is also studied experimentally in artificial conditions on tasks that are nonsensical to animals, and the results are extrapolated to humans.)[3]

All this emphasis on nonsense was done in the name of science, constrained by the rules of "experimental control." In other words, experimental psychologists deliberately studied contrived learning, the most difficult of all kinds of learning. It was contrived learning that made experimental psychology's laboratory studies of learning possible. The studies were ruined if subjects were able to make any kind of sense of the nonsense, if the nonsense syllables reminded them of real words, especially if the words could be combined in some way to make a little story or a description of a scene, no matter how bizarre. The experimenters were not interested in meaningful learning—it was too individualistic and unpredictable. If subjects took control from experimenters by finding some way of comprehending what was to be learned, the only thing that could be predicted was that learning became very much faster; the experiment was ruined.

Subjects were not allowed to "think" during these laboratory experiments. The use of nonsensical materials permitted the artificial separation of learning and thinking. Any meaningful or thoughtful learning that subjects did during experiments was ignored completely. Subjects were regarded as not having learned very much if they learned only a few items on the list, no matter how much they learned about the nature of the experiment, the furnishings of the room they were in, and the appearance of the experimenters.

Because experimental psychology's theories of learning were based on "scientific" laboratory studies, they appealed to those educators who tended, like experimental psychologists, to see learning in terms of control. Psychology even looked as if it could guarantee learning, provided there was sufficient "time on task." It became taken for granted that learning should be difficult and basically incomprehensible to the learner, requiring time, effort, and tedium.

Something experimental psychologists did not talk about so persuasively to educators was that their learning curve was inexorably followed by a forgetting curve, which fell just as steeply as the beginning of the learning curve rose. Most forgetting, the researchers observed, took place immediately after the last learning trial, and without continual repetition and practice everything was likely to be soon forgotten. There was experimental evidence, in other words, that nonsense learning—the rote memorization of lists of arbitrarily selected and unrelated items—was the most inefficient way to learn, a way that guaranteed forgetting. Meaningfulness—the possibility of thinking about what was being learned—was what made learning stick.

But once again, the course of forgetting was predictable only if the subjects were required to learn nonsense. With meaningful learning, experimental results were no longer "lawful" and predictable. The only thing that was predictable when subjects could make a little sense of what they were required to learn—when some thinking crept into the situation—was that forgetting, if it took place at all, was very much slower.[4]

The conclusion that many experimental psychologists ignored and that many educators have found difficult to tolerate is that learning is easiest when external control is relaxed, when individuals (or their brains) are permitted to take charge of their own learning. Learning is prolific when it is unfettered in any way, when it is not contrived.

Learning and Thinking

Learning is not something that is done separately from thinking—except under the experimental laboratory conditions (or controlled classroom conditions) that I have just described. Inferring, concluding, deciding, and solving problems are inseparable from learning. We do not draw an inference and then learn; we learn as we draw the inference. We do not reach a conclusion and then learn the conclusion that we have reached; the learning and the conclusion occur together. To solve a problem is to learn to solve the problem. Learning without thinking would be pointless—what would be learned? But thinking without learning is impossible. The learning is inevitable; it is common-place.

Learning and thinking are not carried on consecutively, or even simultaneously by different parts of the brain. They are not like rubbing our stomach with one hand and patting our head with the other. We learn in the course of thinking. We think while we read a newspaper or watch a movie—it is impossible to do either without thinking—and learning takes place concurrently.

We even learn when we find something difficult to think about. If we are confused in a particular kind of situation, then we learn that such situations are confusing. If we are intimidated in a particular situation, then we learn that such situations are intimidating. We not only learn about situations, we learn how we feel about situations; we never forget an emotional response. If a certain kind of problem makes us feel inadequate and frustrated, we can learn always to feel inadequate and frustrated in the face of that kind of problem.

Learning is not a seal of approval that we stamp on particular thoughts and feelings that we want to stay with us in the future. Rather, learning is the aspect of thinking that carries us into the future. There is no point in thinking about anything with reference only to the present or the past. Thinking is always oriented to the future, to what might take place—or to what we might prefer not to take place—on future occasions. Even if we are solely concerned with what might take place in the next few moments in our existence, our thoughts must still be projected into the future. Learning is not the preparation of a repertoire of knowledge or skills that might be useful in time to come; it is simply the future implications of current thought.

REMEMBERING, UNDERSTANDING, LEARNING, AND THINKING

It may now seem that I have trapped myself in a massive contradiction, in a logical impossibility. At various points in this chapter I have said that the brain is remembering, understanding, learning, and thinking all the time, usually without effort or our awareness, and usually with remarkable efficacy. How can the brain do four things at once? Does it switch between doing one thing and another with lightning speed and efficiency, like a "multitasking" computer? Or is the brain a "parallel processing device," able to perform a number of different operations simultaneously? Neither alternative is the answer, because in fact there is no problem. The brain is not doing four things at once when we remember, understand, learn, and think. It is doing one.

Remembering, understanding, learning, and thinking are not different mental activities, processes, or collections of skills. To think they are is to make a fundamental categorization error. Just because the four different words exist does not mean they refer to four different mental processes or sequences of events, no matter how familiar and distinctive the words might be. The fact that researchers may conduct different kinds of studies under the four headings does not mean they are studying four different things (though the way they conduct experimental studies may make remembering, understanding, learning, and thinking look like different things). The fact that educators organize the curriculum, instructional materials, tests, and the school day itself in terms of remembering, comprehension, learning, and thinking does not mean that these are different things. The researchers and educators are not thinking about people when they establish their categories; they are thinking about the words.

We have different words for remembering, understanding, learning, and thinking simply to reflect different perspectives or points of view. The different words exist in commonplace language not because of something distinctive going on in a person's head, but because of something distinctive that can be seen or imagined to be taking place in the world. When people are most conspicuously thinking about the past, we say they are *remembering.* If their thinking is directed to the present, we call it *understanding.* Future consequences of thinking we call *learning.* It is like the blind scholars and the elephant; depending on the direction of their attention, they believe they are confronted by a snake, a wall, or a treetrunk. Depending on the part of human mental life we focus attention on, it can look like remembering, understanding, learning, or thinking. But these are all different aspects, different reflections, of a single, continual, undifferentiated event—the brain at work, going about its own affairs.

4

IMAGINATION

Imagination is constantly underrated. The brain is not usually given much credit for imaginativeness, except when we are being conspicuously "artistic" or "inventive." Excursions of the imagination are often considered to be a waste of time, distraction, escapes from reality—irresponsible even. Fantasizing, daydreaming, and talking to ourselves may be regarded as indulgent if not reprehensible private activities.

But imagining is something else that the brain does continually. Far from being an escape from reality, imagination makes reality possible. For once, the dictionary provides a reasonable description of what the brain is doing when imagination is defined as the forming of mental concepts of what is not actually present to the senses, the mental consideration of actions or events not yet in existence, and the conception of the absent as if it were present. In short, imagination is the creation of possible realities, including the reality we actually inhabit.

CREATING REALITY

The brain has no direct contact with the physical world in which we live; the world is never actually present to the senses. The eyes are not "windows" through which an inner eye can gaze at objective truth, nor do the eyes send images of reality back to the brain to be observed. There is no inner eye to examine such images. The brain is secluded in the dark and soundproof vault of the skull, with no sensory organs of its own and no contact with the outside world except for the barrages of neural impulses it receives from (and sends to) the eyes, ears, skin, and every other sensory organ. And these neural impulses are totally undifferentiated—the waves of bioelectrical energy constantly flowing along the fibers of the optic nerve, between the eyes and the brain, are no different in quality or form from those found in the auditory nerve between the ears and the brain, or in any other bundle of nerve fibers. It is difficult to avoid calling all this neural activity *messages* or *information*, but the terms are quite inappropriate. *Clues* might be a better word. How can the brain receive messages from a place where it has never been, to which it has no direct access, which it can understand only through the imposition of its own understanding? This is a profound and unresolved philosophical enigma (not helped by the fact that the brain's own existence is part of the "objective" world that we have to assume the brain itself creates).

The brain does not respond or react to the world; it creates the world. Whatever is "out there" receives its form and substance from the brain itself. All texture and meaningfulness that we perceive in the world around us are put there by the brain, order imposed on chaos. The brain paints the images that we see, composes the sounds that we hear, and shapes the substances that we feel. The brain creates the world we call *reality*—with the same imaginative sweep that creates the other worlds we call *fantasy*.[1]

The brain also has no direct contact with what we call *the present*. There is no razor-sharp ridge of the "here and now" on which we can stand to view receding horizons of the past in one direction and advancing vistas of the future in the other. Our present expands or contracts to fit the space we make available for it, perhaps only a few moments (but still a passage of time) if we are experiencing a particular event, but many days or even weeks if we are reflecting on "our present situation." We live in the past and the future, both products of our imagination, as we constantly revise our own history and anticipate what is to come. We view the present from the perspectives of the past and future, and, like the past and the future, the present is a product of our imagination.

We would not have reality without fantasy; reality is a fantasy that works. Imagination permeates every aspect of our lives. We could not get through the day without imagination. It is at the heart of everything we do. We even imagine, extending and contracting, the space occupied by our own bodies. When we are handwriting, our fingers end at the point of the pencil or pen. If we are sweeping a floor, our arms end at the bristles of the broom. When we drive, our bodies expand to encompass the fenders of the car (and we wince when something approaches them). Connect us electronically to a robot, so that its arms move when our arms move and we see what is in front of its eyes, and we feel that we have entered the body of the robot (Moravec, 1988).

Imagination is not something to which we must deliberately turn our mind; it is the fundamental condition of the brain. The moment we relax attention to anything, fantasy takes control. Distraction is the imagination going off in a direction of its own. The subjects in sensory-deprivation experiments, enveloped in cottonwool on the softest of mattresses in dark and sound-proofed rooms, do not fall asleep when denied all sensory stimulation. With their minds unfettered by objective reality, they have psychedelic experiences, hallucinate, and visit new worlds.

The brain is not an information-processing device, any more than it is a passive, reactive device. The brain does not seek or respond to information in the world—the brain *imposes* meaningfulness on the world. It is an active, experience-seeking, reality-creating organ. The enormous quantity of knowledge that we accumulate as we go through life is not the purpose of life but a byproduct of experience. We learn the worlds we create. The brain is constantly *generating* possibilities of realities that may or may not exist objectively, and our experience of these realities constitutes our life and our identity.

Louise Rosenblatt (1978) distinguishes two main reasons for reading: one is for information (when we would be just as content not to read at all, to get the information in some other way), and the other is for experience (when we savor the reading, read the same passages several times, and would be offended if someone tried to save us the trouble by telling us the ending). The same distinction applies to life itself. There may be times when we look for information, but we try to get that kind of chore out of the way as quickly and effortlessly as possible. Most of the time we seek experience, which we usually do not want to be deprived of by other people. We rarely want facts to take the place of living.

Our imaginary realities are furnished with the same basic structures and relationships as those found in the world around us, not because our imaginations are limited to what we have experienced, but because experience is constrained by what we can imagine.

Constructing an internal image of the world in which we live—together with all manner of mental maps, diagrams, catalogs, representations, and descriptions—is a minor concern for human brains, boring and futile. There is little we can do about the world as it is at the moment, about the here and now. We are constantly thinking of the world as it might have been in the past, and how it could be in the future. We relive events of the past, the pleasant and the unpleasant, as they were and as we wish they had been. We invent new pasts. We anticipate events in the future, as we think they might be, as we wish they might be, as we know they never could be. We remember our futures. For recreation—and for re-creation—we live in the imaginary worlds that we and the world's artists construct.

REALITIES OF THE IMAGINATION

In our reading, in plays and movies, and in the theater of our own mind, we make excursions into the worlds of other people—past, present, and future; "factual" and fictional. We constantly look for new lives to live, new landscapes to explore, not because we want to escape the real world, but because these alternative worlds have the same compelling reality for us. (Rather than wanting to escape *from* the real world, we may occasionally need to escape *into* its routines and constraints, to evade demands and anxieties of the imagination.)

All worlds of the imagination are realities, including our dreams and our play.[2] They are realities in the sense that they relate directly to our cognitions and emotions; they do not "represent" anything else. We interpret these imagined worlds in the same terms, respond to them with the same feelings, and remember them in the same ways. Events of the past can bring tears to the eyes or joy to the heart, whether they were actual events, a movie we saw, an illustration in a book, something we read, or just pure fantasy—a compelling daydream we used to have. The brain does not differentiate these various kinds of events as different kinds of experience, either when they occur or in retrospect. They are all experience, and if we are to remember whether the different events "actually" took place or were "simply imagined" we have to attach the appropriate tag to them—a tag that often seems to get lost over time.

All of these worlds have the same ingredients, whether we experience them in "reality," in books, plays, or movies, in art, or in personal fantasy. We understand them in terms of the reality in which we ourselves live, which we ourselves construct. We perceive fictitious objects with familiar uses, fictitious landscapes with familiar possibilities (or with familiar obstacles), and fictitious people with familiar intentions. We relate everything to ourselves, not in arbitrary or abstract ways, but as connected elements of coherent experience.

There are no categories of experience that are exclusive to the physical world, to literature, or to art. Any understanding or meaningfulness that we can find in the objective world we can also find in books and art. Any insights that we can derive from literature or art can be applied to the physical world and to the worlds of our own fantasy. All of these experiences in the different worlds relate to exactly the same emotions— we do not have one way of feeling about the physical world and other ways to feel about the worlds that we imagine or that others imagine for us. To the brain, to imagination, all sources of experience are just one interrelated world in which we live, find stories, and invest emotions.

The imagination constantly strives to discover, to explore, to create explanations and meaningfulness—and it does all this indiscriminately, in the real world and in the worlds of literature, art, and personal fantasy. The alternative is boredom, the absence of meaningful experience, which is universally intolerable. To think, to imagine and experience all possible worlds, is to know we are alive.

The realities the imagination creates also make sense of our life. Culture—a social product of the imagination—is inseparable from the reality that the world presents to us; it is every society's way of constructing its own shared world. The "real world" constantly imposes itself on us, but culture tells us what that reality is. We cannot recognize something as a tree unless our culture has already taught us what a tree is, not just the name, but everything we know about trees.

To give something a name says nothing, unless the name already has meaning for us. Names do not help us to make sense of the world, only the meanings we make of the names. And we are forever trying to give meanings to the words that name aspects of our experience. The semantic complexity of all the words related to thinking illustrates the dual urge to differentiate through naming and to find meanings behind names. We put names to matters that we do not understand and invest those names with potent meanings. Long before people agreed on the physical features of the earth, different cultures in their own ways had charted heaven and hell (Boorstin, 1985, chapter 10).

Cultures constrain human imagination within social bounds. Culture does not take the place of the imagination; it is a product of the imagination, and imagination is still required to make sense of it. Culture ensures that everyone within the same group constructs a similar reality, seeing the world the same way. Art ensures that new realities are always possible.

SPECIFICATIONS OF IMAGINATION

There would seem to be no limit to the realities that the brain can generate and in which it can believe. These realities are comprehensive rather than exhaustive. We never know everything about a world, even the limited world in which we intimately move. There is always room to learn more—or to imagine more—about the world. Nevertheless we rarely have the feeling that our knowledge is incomplete because the parts that we know are mutually coherent, compactly integrated. This is the reason infants are rarely confused by new events in their lives, no matter how limited their accumulated experience might be. New knowledge enriches the old rather than extending or supplanting it.

We may feel that we remember an entire scene, when reflection would show us that many of the parts are missing from our perception and memory. We anticipate an event, but introspection demonstrates that many of the details are not filled in. The imagination often does not concern itself with *detail* in its creations; detail would usually be inadequate and confining. Instead the imagination composes broad *specifications*, which can accommodate all kinds of contingencies and variations. The mind's specifications are like the specifications of a house, which set out the *kind* of edifice to be constructed but do not determine in advance what the final product will be like. Many different kinds of building will satisfy the same requirements. Authors and artists do not wait to have every detail and brushstroke of what they are about to do in place in their mind. As long as what they produce conforms to the outline with which they began, or as it was modified on the way, then they can say "This is what I have in mind"—even though quite different alternatives would conform to the same expectations.

All our intentions and expectations about the world are generated by the imagination in the form of specifications. We rarely set out in advance precisely what we would like to achieve, nor do we anticipate exactly what is likely to happen. Neither course would be particularly productive. But as long as what transpires is congruent with the general pattern we had in mind, we can consider that our desires have been met or our predictions fulfilled.

IMAGINATION, REMEMBERING, UNDERSTANDING, AND LEARNING

Psychologists have long recognized the ubiquity of imagination, at least indirectly, although usually without giving imagination its due. Memory, psychologists frequently point out, is *constructive*; we never recall what actually happened, but only what we now think must have happened. We can be quite persuaded that a particular event took place in the past when it did not, and we can be equally convinced of the reverse. We can remember an incident without being able to remember whether we were present, or read about it, or saw it in a movie. Eyewitnesses are notoriously unreliable sources of courtroom evidence. Demagogues exploit the imagination of their followers in order to manipulate their memories. Imagination is inextricably mingled with memory, and with our understanding of the past. But without imagination, we could have no memory at all.

Our memories demonstrate that imagination can never be separated from feelings. Psychologists say that memory is "state dependent." If we are happy we tend to remember, to reconstruct, happy events from the past. When depressed, we are more likely to call depressing occasions to mind. It is often our feelings about past events that we can recall most accurately, in the most detail. Imagination puts images to our feelings, and our feelings drive the imagination.

Psychologists also assert that our understanding of the present is based on *anticipation*. We do not wait for something to happen in order to make sense of it. We anticipate what will happen (within a range of likely alternatives), and provided what happens matches something in our range of expectations, in the specification, then that is what we perceive. Life depends on prediction—we would never cross the street if we could not predict whether we would be hit by oncoming traffic. Comprehension of language is based on prediction. Individual words have so many possible meanings and applications that we would never understand what anyone says without a prior expectation of what they are trying to say. But rigidly fixed meanings or definitions would make communication impossible, because words would rarely be specifically applicable and comprehensible in a wide range of circumstances. Unambiguous languages are only useful in limited contexts where there can be no room for relative interpretations, such as knitting patterns, computer programming, and mathematics. Language, and the world, are understood through prediction—and prediction is the imagination at work.

Impressed by the effortless fluency and speed with which children, almost unaided, untangle the complexities of the way people around them speak, psychologists have proposed that children *invent* language. Children do not invent new languages, but rather the particular language that they learn. They generate hypotheses about how the language they hear about them works, and they learn from whether or not their hypotheses are substantiated. Other psychologists, trying to account for the enormous amount children succeed in learning about language and the world in their early years, have characterized them as "experimenters" and "hypothesis testers." And invention, once again, is the imagination at work.

Indeed it could be said that remembering, understanding, and learning are just different ways of looking at the imagination, or of talking about it. When we look at imagination from a past-tense perspective, we talk of memory. Comprehension is imagination in the present tense, and learning is imagination from the viewpoint of the future. There is no need to postulate separate "remembering," "compre-hension," and "learning" processes in the brain. They are simply imagi-nation, perceived and discussed from different vantage points.[3]

IMAGINATION AND THINKING

Still from a grammatical point of view, comprehension might be seen as imagination in an objective mood, focused on actuality, while thinking is a subjunctive mood, concerned with hypothetical or contin-gent events. An original and now-archaic use of the term *imagination* was to denote thinking; thinking and imagining were not distinguished.

David Perkins, co-director of the Harvard Graduate School of Edu-cation's extensive *Project Zero* study into artistic thinking (zero was an estimate of how much was known about the topic at the beginning), published an article entitled "Reasoning as Imagination" (Perkins, 1985). Rather than being alternative modes of thinking, which Perkins thought was the way reasoning and imagining were often considered, he concluded there was no difference between them. There could be no reasoning without imagination, nor imagination without reasoning— and the best reasoners always exercised the most imagination.[4]

In a reflective book on the thought and learning of children and adults, entitled *Actual Minds, Possible Worlds*, Bruner (1986) concludes that imagination is the basis of all science, literature, and philosophy— and of everyday experience and the "self" as well.[5]

However thinking is regarded, it cannot be distinguished from imagination, from "possible worlds" or realities. Problems are solved when relationships are perceived that were not evident before. Deci-sions are made when new states of affairs are considered to be more appropriate than the present state. Inferences are drawn when one state of affairs is related to another. Intuition and insight both refer to the perception of relationships, of possibilities and intentions, that are not directly evident.

Imagination and action are inseparable. No activity is undertaken without an image of the result (even if a particular consequence is falsely anticipated). We take a walk to achieve some imagined state of affairs at the end of the walk (or during the walk, if we are walking for the sake of the walk itself). Artists and athletes practice ideal perfor-mances by imagining ideal performances. Problems are solved by vi-sualizing how a solution might look. Intentions drive all behavior, and our intentions are always imagined outcomes. If we sometimes wonder why we are doing something, it is because our imagination has been occupied with something else, not because we have stopped thinking altogether. It is impossible to discuss thinking, from any point of view, without employing terms that involve the imagination. We imagine all the time, effortlessly, inconspicuously, and effectively, in the same way that we continually think, remember, comprehend, and learn.[6]

When we say someone has no imagination, we are speaking metaphorically, using a figure of speech, like saying someone is dead from the neck up. No one can be devoid of imagination, although their imagination can drive them in ways that might be called unimaginative. Their imagination can tell them that there is only one world worth inhabiting, and that is the small, controlled, secure world in which they constrain themselves. Their imagination can populate the regions beyond that world with demons and dangers, so that their bodies and behavior will never roam outside their self-imposed bounds. Such people are shackled by their own imagination—they imagine they are unimaginative, and feel happier that way.

THE DYNAMO OF THE BRAIN

I have argued that the brain can imagine, remember, comprehend, learn, and think simultaneously. How is it possible for the brain to do five different things at once? There can be only one answer: They are not different things. I proposed in the previous chapter that remembering, understanding, and learning are indistinguishable from thinking, and now I am suggesting that thinking and imagination are the same. We may talk about them in different ways, as if they are different, but that is because the words we choose are always influenced by the context in which we talk or write. It makes sense to differentiate whether we are imagining something, remembering something, learning something, understanding something, or thinking about something, but that differentiation is related to the situation, or to the perspective of the person we are addressing, not to something different going on in the brain.

It is impossible for us to do these five things separately, or just part of the time. We do not think for a while, then perhaps remember something, then understand, then learn, and occasionally use our imagination. As you read these sentences, you are not rapidly switching between remembering, understanding, learning, thinking, and imagining. If you are able to understand what I am saying at all, you must be doing all those things simultaneously; they must be one all-embracing continual brain activity. And the power behind that one activity must be imagination.

I have also talked about remembering, understanding, learning, and thinking as being easy "as long as the brain is in control of its own affairs." Now I can explain what that expression means. Remembering, understanding, learning, and thinking are easy as long as the imagination is in control, when the brain is pursuing a course determined by its own imagination. Remembering, understanding, learning, and thinking are simply byproducts of the imagination, bound to take place if the imagination is active. Remembering, understanding, learning, and thinking become difficult only when they are "contrived," when the imagination is not in charge, or not even involved. The brain without the imagination in control is like a runaway vehicle.

Imagination is the dynamo of the brain, the source of all our intellectual energy and creativeness. As long as the imagination generates its power, we remember, understand, learn, and think, smoothly and efficiently, at least within the constraints established by the imagination itself. But when there is an override on the imagination, when our thinking is directed in some other way, such as an arbitrary decision by ourselves or someone else, then all operations fail. The brain loses its integrity (in both senses of the word), it is thrown out of gear, and every facet of thinking is shattered.

5

PATTERNS AND STORIES

Every dynamo requires a governor to prevent it from running out of control. Flywheels can generate so much energy that they leave their bearings and destroy everything around, including the machinery they power. What prevents the imagination, the dynamo of the brain, from running out of control, so that we confuse fantasy with reality, or experience only a kaleidoscope of disorganized sensory impressions?

Right now, as I sit at my desk, I can imagine I am 2,000 miles away on a tropical beach, ready to dive into the inviting ocean. Since imagination is also the basis of the reality I currently inhabit, what prevents my imagination running amok so that I think I really am on a beach, and dive off my chair onto the floor? If the imagination can generate all kinds of possibilities, how do we select the most appropriate one at any particular time? What keeps the imagination within bounds?

There is a governor that controls the imagination, but there is no familiar name for it because we are not normally aware of its existence or operation. It is not something we often talk about. The manner in which the imagination is kept within useful bounds is *pattern-recognition*. We have a continual and remarkable facility to look for and find patterns in everything we encounter. In fact, pattern-recognition is something else that everyone's brain is routinely superbly good at (unless, once again, there is severe neurological impairment), without effort or even conscious awareness.

Pattern-recognition is involved in every aspect of life, in every sensory modality. But it is perhaps the most striking, and has been most studied, in relation to visual perception, the way we *see* the familiar world.

IMPOSING ORDER ON VISUAL CHAOS

How is it we are able to recognize our friends almost every time we encounter them? We rarely see them in the same way twice. They change their clothes, and we encounter them in different settings, in different lights, from different angles. A brief glimpse of someone's back may be sufficient for us to recognize a friend at another table in a dimly lit restaurant. What we look at may be chaotic, but what we see is orderly. What do we know that enables us to make rapid and usually accurate recognitions? What do we have in the brain that makes them possible?

The answer, as I have pointed out, is not photographic images. There is no eye in the brain. We do not compare the person we are looking at with a collection of snapshots that we have stored away in the brain. How could we have an internal image to compare with every conceivable circumstance in which we might see our friends, including circumstances in which we have never seen them before? Instead, we appear to compare some kind of *description* of the person we are looking at with a description that we ourselves generate of what the person might or should look like. And provided the descriptions match to our satisfaction, that is the person we see. We do not necessarily see the person in front of our eyes; we see the person we decide is in front of our eyes (occasionally making a mistake), depending on how well the descriptions match and how well we expect (or want) them to. In other words, perception involves complex thinking.

We may also see more than is actually in front of the eyes (or think we see more, which is the same thing). If we decide that the person we glimpse in the gloom is our friend, we *see* that person clearly, imagining detail that may not be present to our eyes. This is part of the "in-filling" that I discussed in examining the feeling that we perceive a complete scene, in the real world or in a picture, when in fact the imagination paints in many of the details or takes for granted that the details are there. We do not see what is in front of our eyes, but rather an imaginative image derived from our expectation—our specifications—of what we are looking at. Our eyes must provide evidence for the expectation, and the evidence may be very slight indeed.

Pattern-recognition ensures that we normally see meaningful patterns rather than unrelated episodes and that what we see bears some resemblance to what is going on. But pattern-recognition still leaves the imagination a good deal of freedom. The products of the imagination are what mathematicians call a *bounded infinity*, like the set of prime numbers. There is no limit to the total number of them, but there are restrictions on what they may be.

The theory of person-perception that I have just outlined has not been investigated to any great extent by experimental psychologists, nor has there been much research into how we are able to distinguish tables from chairs, knives from forks, birds from aircraft, or any of the multitude of different kinds of objects that we are able to recognize on sight. The problem, from a research point of view, is too overwhelming; our perceptions are too abundant for any current theory to explain in detail. But a seemingly less complex aspect of visual pattern-recognition has received considerable attention—and provided me with the framework of the "description-matching" hypothesis I have just outlined. It is known as *letter recognition*, concerned with how we are able to recognize the alphabet.[1]

What have we learned when we can distinguish the different letters? It is not enough to say that we have learned what each letter looks like or that we have learned the shape of each letter (although these are both part of the right answer), because the basic issue is still unsolved—what do we know that enables us to recognize a shape? What is in our head to correspond to the shapes that we focus our eyes upon?

The answer once again is not a picture, an image, or a "template" of every letter of the alphabet. We can recognize letters of the alphabet in forms we have never met before—thin letters and fat, tall letters and short, upright and italic, boldface and light, with embellishments and without, chiseled, shadowed, in reverse, in a variety of sizes, in different colors, on different kinds of surface. We can identify letters in a multiplicity of handwriting styles, or when they are traced on the soles of our feet with a finger. How do we do it?

Researchers have dismissed template theories—the idea that we have a variety of images of what letters might look like stored in the brain. Template systems cannot account for the versatility of human letter-recognizers, even very young children. (On the other hand, template systems are the only ones that work reliably for computers. Computers must be programmed with exact representations of what letters or numbers look like. But then computers can only recognize letters and numbers that look exactly like the images they have been programmed with; they cannot *think*.)

Researchers have proposed a *feature-analytic* hypothesis for human letter-recognition involving the entire visual system, eyes and brain together. In essence, the brain employs the eyes to look for specific "features" of letters, according to prior expectations about what letters should look like. The features can be regarded as buildingblocks out of which letters are made, such as straight lines and curves in various orientations. The features can also include relational attributes such as whether the forms are open (like *c*) or closed (like *o*); symmetrical (like *w*) or asymmetrical (like *b*). If the eyes detect features that the brain considers appropriate to the letter *a*, then we see an *a*, but if the brain thinks the features more appropriate to the letter *e*, then an *e* is seen (even if we are looking at an *a*).

What the brain has stored away, according to feature-analytic theory, is not alternative images of what every letter of the alphabet looks like, but one or more descriptions of what each letter *could* look like, of how each letter is constructed, and of how features are combined. The descriptions come from the imagination; we construct them ourselves. They are like the *specifications* I have already referred to; they are patterns of expectations.

The act of learning to recognize a particular letter, say the letter *g*, goes something like this. The first time we encounter a letter that we know is a *g*, we do not try to memorize what a *g* looks like. Instead we imagine how such a letter might be constructed. We form a specification of how a *g* might be put together, a tentative feature list. The next time we encounter a letter that might be *g*, we recognize it if it looks the way a *g* we would construct would look. If we make a mistake, recognizing a letter as *g* when we should not have done so, we revise our feature list. And if we fail to recognize a *g* because it does not correspond with our particular specification for the letter, such as *G*, we construct an alternative specification.

We recognize faces, letters of the alphabet, and everything else that is familiar to us if the description of the visual world we receive from the eyes satisfies a description that we ourselves generate, in our mind's eye, so to speak. Neither of those descriptions is in the form of words, of course. The "description" that we generate is a potential image, and if the match is made, the image is what we see. The pattern-recognizer is *selective;* it chooses among the alternatives that the imagination generates and keeps the imagination under control.

To say we construct possible letters in the imagination does not mean we could reproduce them precisely ourselves. We recognize letters in forms we could not possibly produce in our own handwriting. This is writing with the imagination, not with the hand. It is extremely difficult, often impossible, as we all know, to draw things that we can easily reproduce (or produce) with the mind. I can recognize my friend's face, I can remember it well, but I cannot draw it, not because there is something defective about the way I perceive the face, but because I am a poor artist. In the mind we can paint entire worlds, but very few of us have the talent to do the same on canvas.

The imagination creates the possibility of visual experience, but pattern-recognition ties what we see to the real world. We can imagine a sunlit beach, but unless the scene we are looking at generates a description compatible with our specification for a beach, we do not see a beach. To see the beach in the mind, we have to close the eyes, or close our minds to our eyes. We do not usually confuse fantasy with reality, even though imagination is the basis of both, because we usually know whether we are using our eyes or not. Pattern generation is going on all the time, but when we are looking at the objective world we look for confirming evidence.[2]

Occasionally imagination misleads us, and we see things that are not actually in front of the eyes—because we have little evidence, or great hopes, or can tolerate our life in no other way. But generally, pattern-recognition ties imagination to reality. Reality does not "stimulate" perception; it confirms it.

OTHER PATTERNS

Theories of pattern-recognition are not restricted to vision. Psychologists borrowed the feature-analytic hypothesis for visual perception from a linguistic theory devised to account for the understanding of speech. The speech-recognition problem is similar to the sight one: We never experience exactly the same phenomenon twice, so how are we able to recognize anything as the same?

How do we recognize the words that other people utter? No two people speak in the same way (voices are almost always distinguishable on the telephone), yet we recognize particular words as the same even when they are uttered by different people. And we utter them in yet another way ourselves. How do we manage to do it?

Take a particular case. A baby hears one adult pronounce the word *milk* in a soprano voice, while another adult says it in a baritone. Brother drawls the word, and sister clips it short. And when the baby says the word, it does so in another way again. Spectrographic analysis of the formant frequencies in the different ways of uttering the word may show that they have little in common, so the baby learning the word clearly is not "imitating" or "copying" the sounds that other people make, not in any passive or mechanical sense. Instead, the infant analyzes *features* of every word that is learned. These features are aspects of the way the sound is produced—the shape of the mouth, the configuration of the tongue and lips, the nature of the breathing, and the tension of the vocal cords. Our memory of words is a memory of the way we would produce them ourselves, and we recognize words when acoustic events occur in the world that match the descriptions, the specifications, that the imagination generates. Researchers call this *analysis by synthesis*. We recognize patterns in speech by generating for ourselves possibilities of what we are listening to and checking whether reality confirms our expectations. We recognize sounds by the manner in which we would produce those sounds ourselves (with the imagination, not necessarily with the voice).

The sounds of speech are produced in the mind of the listener. When acoustic events take place in ambiguous circumstances, we are likely to hear anything as our imagination takes over. We do not hear what is happening; we hear what we *think* is happening. The wind rustling through the trees at night becomes voices. There is a muttering from the next room, and we imagine we can detect the language that is being used, and occasional words, even though we may not hear enough to understand what is being said. We impose our beliefs and expectations on uncertainty, in the world of sounds as well as the world of sight. We cannot experience anything we cannot imagine, and imagination is normally kept under control by our search for meaningful patterns. The patterns that we recognize, in sight or in sound, are patterns that we ourselves produce.

The same applies to other sensory modalities, to all our senses. We do not respond to raw chemical events in taste or smell, but rather to complex relationships and meaningful interpretations that we impose on the phenomena. It is difficult to tell whether we like the taste or smell of something when our eyes are blindfolded—we need to *know* what confronts us before we can sense it accurately. Eating in the dark is usually not appetizing. The same applies to touch, in all its complexity. We have to know what we are touching before we can tell how we feel about touching it. If we do not know what we are touching, our imagination takes over completely and makes an identification for us, reassuring or terrifying, imposing reality on what would otherwise be chaotic, meaningless occurrences.

We rarely experience chaos, in the sense of meaningless, uninterpretable incidents, a "formless void." (When we say that a situation is "chaotic," we usually mean that it is out of control, rather than that it is inexplicable.) Artists who try to depict chaos have to employ conventions—and they still cannot prevent audiences from imposing meaning on what they do. Normally we make sense out of everything that is going on around us by projecting patterns of orderliness to create a meaningful world. Our search for meaningful patterns keeps the imagination under control.[3]

Common sense was originally postulated as the sense required to link all the other senses together, a sense that is common to all our experience. It is not enough to recognize sights, sounds, smells, tastes, or tactile patterns; we need to integrate all those diverse sensory elements into coherent, meaningful experiences. We do not live in parallel worlds of sight, sound, smell, and so forth, but in a single unified world with distinctive sights, sounds, and smells. Something has to unite these different domains of experience, and that is the role for which a "common sense" was proposed, a sense that made sense of everything else. When I talk about the brain "creating reality," I am referring to an overall integrating principle that once would have been called *common sense*. (Even today, in one sense, *common sense* refers to this overall construction of our individual worlds. We say something is contrary to common sense when it does not accord with the world that we ourselves have created and believe in.)

PATTERNS IN TIME

The pattern-generating and pattern-recognizing creativity of the brain is also required to make sense of temporal events. Most of the experiences that we have in our lives are extended in time, and there has to be some way of linking successive parts of them into coherent wholes. We would never make sense of a movie, a conversation, or a football match—let alone an entire world—if we could not tie together in meaningful ways incidents occurring at different times.

The brain has a remarkable ability to orchestrate occurrences that are extended over time—and no one has the faintest idea of how it is done. After over a hundred years, researchers still have no clue to how a cockroach manages to put one leg after another as it walks. The researchers do not know what to look for in the cockroach's brain. How could intricately organized movement be represented in an organ that has no moving parts?

Everyone has had the experience of switching on a radio, hearing a few notes of music in the middle of a song, and recognizing the song almost as quickly as one becomes aware of the music. How is that done? We do not have magnetic tapes of every song we have ever heard whirring around in our head. And if we did have all those tapes, how would we manage to start playing in our mind the music we are listening to on the radio, at exactly the right point, to make the rapid identification? Computers cannot do this. Once again, no one has the slightest idea how it might be done.

We switch on the television, see a scene in an old movie, and immediately know that we have seen the movie before. We know what is going to happen next. But how do we manage to recognize the movie so rapidly? What goes on in the brain to generate the instant feeling of familiarity? The brain thrives on events, both real and imaginary, that are extended in time. We do not think in isolated snapshots or slices of time, and we do not perceive the world in that way either.

We impose time and movement on static events. We look at a picture of sailboats racing or of runaway horses, and in our mind's eye we see dramatic movement, though the image we are looking at is stationary. We look at a picture of a restaurant scene, and we see people talking and eating, with waiters busily in attendance. We do not see arrested movement. We cannot avoid experiencing activity, even when it is not actually occurring. When the picture is of a motionless person or animal, we inject life and movement into it. We say, "The portrait was so realistic, I almost saw the person breathing." We observe a succession of slightly changing stationary images on a movie screen, and we see a smooth and continually developing series of events. Time and movement are other patterns that the brain generates and imposes on chaos. The imagination is kept under control because we expect events to occur in predictable and customary ways, not arbitrarily or randomly—or statically.

There is yet another kind of pattern that the human brain continually organizes and projects in order to maintain a meaningful coherence in real and imagined occurrences. This is the patterning that is imposed on experience itself. We do not perceive the world in terms of isolated and unconnected incidents, but as coherent *events*. Event-ness is not an inherent characteristic of the world; we experience the world in terms of "things going on" because we impose a structure of events on everything. It is rare—and disturbing—for us to encounter successions of incidents that we cannot put together into some meaningful and explanatory whole. When we ask people about their experiences or their plans, they do not provide us with a list of happenings or facts; they tell us about events.[4]

We do not see the world, or think about the world, as successions of unrelated incidents or collections of randomly ordered images, but as sequences of coherent and interconnected events. And, in particular, we see and think about the world in the patterns of *stories*.

THE STORIES BEHIND THOUGHT

Thought flows in terms of stories—stories about events, stories about people, and stories about intentions and achievements. The best teachers are the best storytellers. We learn in the form of stories. We construct stories to make sense of events. Our prevailing propensity to impose story structures on all experience, real or imagined, is the ultimate governor on the imagination, the regulator that keeps it from flying out of control. We even expect our fantasies to make sense. The brain is a story-seeking, story-creating instrument.

I do not have a compact definition of what constitutes a story, or even of how I am using the term. *Story* is another word we all understand in context without being able to put a precise meaning to it. Stories usually but not inevitably involve locations, landscapes, protagonists, intentions, emotions, conflicts, obstacles, struggles, and consequences (which always lead into new stories). These are elements we always look for in any situation in which we are involved.[5]

I include expositions as well as narratives within my use of the word *stories*, "fact" as well as "fiction." These are technical distinctions, not observed by the brain. The key elements in every story are purpose and order. By *purpose* I mean aims and intentions, at least on the part of the author and reader, and usually on the part of characters as well. Stories do things, and things are done in stories. By *order* I mean coherence— the parts are interlocked, with each other and with the actual or imagined reality in which the story takes place. A story is a world that can be entered and explored; it hangs together. (All this is relative, and necessarily so. What is a story to you may not be a story to me if you can make sense of it and I cannot.)

We must all be born with a sense of story in order to make sense of the world, to provide a basis for experience. I am not claiming that we know specific stories when we are born—we have to learn these from the cultures in which we find ourselves. In fact, it might be said that a major function of cultures is to provide and perpetuate the stories that individuals need in order to make sense of the world in which they find themselves.[6]

Cultures teach us the stories by which we will live, but they do not tell us what stories are. How could we begin to comprehend the first stories that we hear, unless we already have an understanding of heroes and villains, right and wrong, good and bad, aims and obstacles, collaboration and conflict, power and prohibition, causes and consequences? We do not have specific foreknowledge of the elements of the particular culture that we embrace; cultures themselves teach us who the heroes and villains will be, and what is good and what is bad. But we must have the prior structures, the *questions*, to which our cultures and our experience provide the detailed answers.

Thinking and Stories

We make up stories about ourselves, usually dramatizing our accomplishments and our difficulties. We want to share many of these stories with other people. They help to confirm the stories we construct about ourselves. We also make up stories about other people; it is the way we understand them. But the story we are probably most interested in, all our life, is the story of the world in which we find ourselves. And we are especially and inevitably interested in the role that we play in this story, the character who is ourself.

We cannot help thinking in terms of stories, whether we are recalling the past, contemplating the present, or anticipating the future. We look at pictures in terms of stories, sometimes in terms of the story of the artist, sometimes in terms of the subject matter, sometimes both. When we say we cannot make sense of something, we mean that we cannot find the story in it or make up a story about it. We look at life in terms of stories, even when there is no story to be told. That is the way we make sense of life: by making stories. It is the way we remember events: in terms of stories. Without stories, there would be no events.

We see two birds on a fence and make up a story about them. We see two colleagues gossiping in a corner and improvise a dialog for them. We never see just people; we see people *doing something,* or planning something, or intending something. We see them in situations, in predicaments. While passing through the crowded lobby of a convention hotel, I overheard a snippet of conversation. One woman was saying to another, "If Fred and I ever split up, I doubt it will be because of a third person." That was all I heard as I walked by—but it is a complete soap opera. It is difficult not to picture Fred, and his relationship with the woman who was talking.

The stories that we construct are not a special way of perceiving the world or of making sense of everything we hear or read. It is the *only* way we can make sense of the world, of literature, and of art; it is also the way our fantasies make sense to us. Stories are our way of perceiving, of conceiving, of creating; they are the way the imagination works. It is no more accurate to assert that life copies art and literature than it is to argue that art and literature reflect life. The plots of life are the plots of literature. They are all cut from the same cloth, the fabric woven into stories by our imagination. No one has to tell us, or teach a child, to perceive life in terms of stories; it is what everyone does. The total of facts and figures that we all collect—a few statistics, telephone numbers, birthdays, addresses—is minuscule compared with all the complex stories contained within the brain.

Our stories are the vantage points from which we perceive the world and the people in it. We anthropomorphize, invest with human personalities, not only animals, but toys, cars, ships, and computers. We give them names, characters, and motives—we see them behaving. We see nations as characters in global dramas. We can be persuaded to fight for nations or other groups as if they were parents or children that we would die—and kill—to defend. We fictionalize "the people," "the government," even "the gods"—and give them roles, often dominant ones, in the stories of our lives.[7]

None of this is a consequence of literacy. Prehistoric humans painted stories on the walls of caves and planned voyages through other lives for the corpses of kings. Unliterate Greeks created, understood, and enjoyed Homeric epics, where gods and men contended.

We all need to know the story we are playing out in our lives. The culture and society to which we adhere give us the framework of that story, the ways in which we interpret the circumstances of our lives. We believe the story because it makes sense to us, from the way we perceive people around us behaving and from the way we see these people perceiving us.

Our stories put the content into the sense of *appropriateness*, or *fitness*, that we all have. Individually we may disagree on what exactly is appropriate, on what is "right and proper," but we all have the strong feeling that certain things are appropriate in particular circumstances and that other things are not. The more plausible we find a story, the better we are able to understand it and recall it (Black, Freeman & Johnson-Laird, 1986). Once again, our culture and personal experience tell us what things are appropriate at particular times, but prior to that must be the expectation that there is such a thing as appropriateness. How could experience teach us that?

An innate sense of appropriateness inevitably implies a sense of the *ridiculous* (not necessarily a separate sense, but simply the converse of appropriateness—everything that is excluded from that category). All individuals have an extremely powerful sensitivity to things that do not belong in their construction of reality. They react strongly to such intrusions; they find them absurd. Everyone has met those irritating people who make social or political comments with which we strongly disagree—and who then laugh to indicate how ludicrous they find any alternative point of view. Why are perceptions of the world different from our own so amusing? What leads people to believe that there are only two points of view, their own and the ridiculous?

The Leading Character

The stories that we believe, and that we use as a basis for our own behavior and attitudes, define our identity, the character we play in our personal story of life. Joseph Campbell (1949) has demonstrated insightfully how humans everywhere build and borrow myths to give meaning to their existence—and have probably done so since human time began.

The universal demand for attention, approval, and acceptance, the insistent "watch me" of children (and adults?) is the delineation of oneself as a leading character in the narrative of life. One might think that with something as central and personal to each of us as our own identity, it would not be necessary to turn to others to validate "who we are." Yet the role we play may be the part of the story we most doubt, the part that others must constantly reassure us about.[8]

Our personal stories—and with them our identity—can fall apart when we lose an important character in our life. And we may spend long periods looking for people to fill certain roles (sometimes too eagerly, putting them into roles that they do not want to play).

We are not content just to compose stories about ourselves and the people in our life. In our minds we produce movies, with ourselves as stars, as heroes or heroines, victors or victims, and we replay excerpts to ourselves, time and time again, constructing a life we may never have, rationalizing a life we may have, and always constructing a reality that makes sense to us. Occasionally we construct multiple, incompatible roles for ourselves, interfering with the life we *have* to have.

OTHER REALITIES

Thought is not restricted to the story-based realities that we construct in the physical world, in flights of fancy, in language and in art, although these realities are the focus of this book. There are other kinds of reality, totally different and quite independent, that the imagination also constructs and experiences, both publicly and in our own minds. These realities can be just as real as the worlds of trees and fishing boats, and they affect the same basic emotions in us; but quite different kinds of event take place in them. They involve different kinds of stories, and we must treat them in different ways cognitively. They are different worlds of experience.

The sketchy treatment that follows is a reflection more of my limited understanding of these alternative realities than of their importance; no book on thought and human behavior should ignore them. They are as much a part of the world in which we live, and of our own mind, as language.

The World of Music

Music is often referred to as a *language*, but the expression is metaphorical. Music is not like speech or written language. I would say that music has a different vocabulary and grammar, except this would be a misleading metaphorical use of the words *vocabulary* and *grammar*. The terminology we use to describe language, the visual arts, or the physical world cannot be used with any precision to talk about music; it is another kind of reality.

It is especially misleading to clump music, language, and the visual arts together because they are all "means of communication." If they are, it is in different ways—not in the representation or expression of information and ideas, but in creating and sharing possibilities of experience. Music opens up possibilities of experience that cannot substitute for—or be substituted by—experience we can have through language, representational pictures and sculpture, or in the physical world. Different media cannot say the same things.

Music is a different kind of reality, a different arena in which thought can create and find experience. We cannot create a storm or a tree in music, except in a figurative sense quite different from the ways storms and trees exist in the world, in language, or in paintings. Music and language are not intertranslatable—a verbal description of a concerto cannot provide a musical experience, nor can a symphony tell the story of a novel.

When music is employed to tell a story, in any detailed sense, it has to combine with other modalities, with visual art in ballet, or with language and visual art in opera or rock videos. In these combinations, music is particularly powerful, multiplying the emotional effect that language and visual art can have.

But music is also powerful in its own right; it appeals directly to human emotions, from excitement and pleasure to sadness and dread. There is no human culture without music, and no culture that music does not profoundly affect.

Our view of the world is largely unconscious, and so is the manner in which we construct it. But we might get some idea of the underlying dynamics by looking at the words of the songs we know well and by thinking critically about much of the music that we hear, often involuntarily. We should always be on guard for the effect on our mood and our thought when there is music in the environment, even when we are scarcely aware of it.

I have been surprised and alarmed by the number of popular songs I still remember from my adolescent years, especially by what I now regard as the insidious words that accompanied the catchy melodies. I do not think that what I learned from those lyrics was always to my benefit. Popular music enculturated me in indelible ways, as it no doubt enculturates young people today with different themes and different messages.

The music of our youth is a particularly effective cement for any kind of memory. The power of rhyme and meter as mnemonic devices has been acknowledged for well over 2,000 years. Until the advent of printed books, important cultural knowledge and beliefs were typically put into rhyming and rhythmic form to facilitate their being remembered.

One can speculate why music and rhyme should be so memorable—because of their predictability, or because of something more fundamental about the responsiveness of human beings to patterns. Commercials and movies aside, I have never seen cats dancing to a tune or cows swaying to a melody. Music appears to be a world that is not accessible to other creatures. Despite stories of the effect of music on milk and egg production, animals do not become involved in music the way humans do. Birds may sing—but that is a metaphorical extension of our language, and they never go to concerts. No animals play instruments. It may in fact be through music and other modes of reality construction, rather than through language, that humans are most easily distinguished from other animals.

Music certainly makes a profound difference to people, and not just to the ones who declare themselves to be "musical." Music is potent in the direct control it exercises over our emotions, and thereby in consolidating the particular ways we think.

Armies the world over march to music—and in peacetime everyone parades to the same tunes, with music exerting its patriotic influence on participants and spectators alike. Every religion has its hymns, and music is a part of most rituals. Politicians and sports promoters employ music to sharpen excitement and enthusiasm and to blunt critical faculties. Music dulls sensitivity to pain, as every dentist knows. Music is used to calm us in the claustrophobia of elevators and put us into a positive spending mode in supermarkets. The most effective television commercials are the ones that best exploit music. Music excites and sedates, heightens the senses and lowers our guard. It is easier to sit through a horror movie if the sound is turned down (and the same movie remains unbearable if we close our eyes but can still hear the music). The music creates more tension than the visual images.

Music constitutes a cosmos of totally different possibilities for humanity, a new galaxy rather than a new world, in which every dimension—time, space, depth, color, harmony—is unique. There are different possibilities for human sensitivity and creativity in the reality that is music. Nothing in space travel could be more dramatic, more absolute, than the changes of reality we experience in our passages from the realms of speech to those of music.

Yet the realities of music are created by the same brains, the same thought potential, that create language and visual art. We respond to them with the same emotions. If we are to understand human thought we must take music into account, even if we cannot account for it. Music is a totally different world that we inhabit—but it is not the only one.

Mathematics, Movement, and Other Realities

There are at least two further realities that we can inhabit, that the human brain can create and experience, that cannot be described or accounted for in the same terms that we use for language, the representational arts, and music.

The first is the world of mathematics, which has its own laws, its own language, and its own mysteries. The way in which mathematics is related to the physical world, except for the very simplest of arithmetic relationships, is unclear. Cosmologists can bring the two together, testing theories about the origins of the universe in abstruse calculation, but they do so by making the universe as incomprehensible to nonmathematicians as mathematics itself.

Mathematicians have difficulty in explaining mathematics, at least to the satisfaction of nonmathematicians. I am not talking about the evident difficulty of teaching mathematics to those "who do not think" in mathematical ways, but about explaining different branches of mathematics, or what they have in common. Some mathematicians say that math is simply a matter of *patterns*—but in the sense in which they (and I) use the term, everything is patterned, from clouds and waves to music and metabolism. Yet not everything is mathematics, not if the word is to have any specific sense. The metaphor does not elucidate what kind of a reality mathematics is.

Classically, mathematics and music have been closely related—the harmonic movements of planetary spheres and the geometry of chords and melodies. But music cannot take the place of astronomy, and mathematical formulae do not sound like symphonies. They are distinct worlds, related more by metaphor than by isomorphic structures. Mathematics can only be explained in terms of mathematics; understanding is more a matter of feeling than of linguistic analysis. Mathematics is yet another kind of reality, another world, that cannot be comprehended from the outside.

There is also a world of movement, independent of the physical world, language and mathematics, that once again requires its own language. Movement has its own rules and relationships, its own essence. It cannot be translated into any other mode of expression, any alternative form of experience. I am talking first of human movement—the joy of engaging in or observing dance, gymnastics, athletics, and many sports, especially when they are well and gracefully done. Movement is infectious; we join in vicariously. To look at movement at its most natural, one must perhaps look at the spontaneity of children. "Maturity" inhibits us.

But we are sensitive to movement not only in ourselves and others. We also respond to movement in nature—to the sway of trees, the rush of the wind, the press of waves against the shore, the cascading of water, the progressions of clouds, even the "harmonies" of successive ranges of mountains. We also respond to mechanical forms of movement—with our hypnotic susceptibility to pendulums and the identification we make with automobiles and bowling balls as we lean in sympathy with the course they are taking, tense in anticipation of the collisions in which they might be involved.

Movement is different from music and mathematics. A different language is required to talk about it (and choreography has proved notoriously difficult to codify). Music, mathematics, and movement are not interchangeable with each other, or with language. A description of a ballet cannot replace a ballet, and one could hardly imagine a piece of music, or a set of mathematical equations, taking the place of a football match. This is not because different feelings are involved—exactly the same feelings are engaged in all the realities thought can create and experience. These realities constitute totally different possibilities of experience.

There are other, more compact realities that we can enter, offering even more possibilities of experience and expression. They are all unique. They need their own language (if we are to talk about them at all), and they provide distinctive kinds of experience, not translatable into each other or into other forms of experience (although once again we respond to them with the same fundamental emotions). These are the worlds of games like chess and bridge, of bookkeeping enterprises like balance sheets and spreadsheets, of the stock exchange, genetic spirals, and particle physics.

The brain does not run out of new worlds to create. The latest and perhaps potentially the most significant new reality is that of computers. Some people find compelling and totally satisfying experiences within computer systems. They explore unique landscapes and use languages totally inaccessible to other people. Like people immersed in music or mathematics, residents of the world of computers live in a different atmosphere, sometimes with only tenuous connections to the commonplace world.

All of these different realities provide thought with fertile domains for expression and experience, extending the power of the imagination. The range of human thought is infinite and awesome. The realities that we are capable of entering are not accounted for by conventional theories of language, art, or perception. They reflect a fundamental propensity of the human brain to invent—and exploit—new possibilities. Thought is relentlessly creative.

6
THINKING CREATIVELY

So far I have been concerned mainly with the brain's imaginative construction of two kinds of reality—the "real world" that imposes itself upon us from outside our body and the alternative worlds that we contemplate in the privacy of our own mind. The first world is a public one, shared with others. It cannot be changed simply by an act of will, though the way we make sense of it, and thus perceive it, is shaped by the imagination. The worlds we create in our head, on the other hand, need never be revealed to others and can be manipulated with ease. These two kinds of reality, public and private, are products of a single imaginative mode of thought continually engaged in by everyone.

There is, however, a third category of reality that can be individually created and personally manipulated but that can also be shared. This kind of reality includes the worlds of art—of painting, literature, and music—constructed by people who behave creatively for others to experience and explore. This is imagination on public view. It is not engaged in by everyone, nor does everyone who tries necessarily do it well. We have entered the domain of "artists," and of "creative thinking."

My topic in this chapter is the noble worlds of music and dance, painting and sculpture, literature, poetry and drama, and all other realms of human ingenuity, like architecture (from garden sheds to ocean liners), design (from letterheads to landscapes), and fabrication (from clothing to cuisine)—all "crafts" and "trades" as well as "arts." I do not have a restrictive definition of the term *art*; there will be sufficient complication in the ways in which the word *creative* is used. My reference is to all the public worlds—to all the potential *experiences*—that would not exist but for the creative efforts of individuals.

Use of the word *creative* as a particular kind of thinking is misleading, although widespread. It suggests that the brain is not normally creative, or that a different kind of mental activity is involved in producing works of art than in thinking generally. Many books have been written on the topic of developing creative thinking. And there are frequent complaints that many people are not as creative as they ought to be, but that special instructional programs could remedy this situation.

Is any of this true? Is anything explained by saying that people have or lack *creativity* (a term I tend to avoid in favor of *creativeness*, which we shall shortly discuss)? Is creative thinking a unique kind of thinking, and is creativeness something that has to be taught? Once more we must begin by considering how language is used, and what might be entailed by the term "creative thinking." When we have a better idea of what is being talked about, we can look at the kind of thinking that is called creative, and how it might be facilitated.

TALKING ABOUT CREATIVENESS

The commonplace creativeness of everyone's imagination is usually ignored when "creative thinking" or "creativity" is discussed. Most people who talk about creative thinking want something more than imaginativeness. There are usually three other requirements: the thinking (or, rather, its observable consequence) must reach *high standards*, it must be *original*, and it must be the result of *intention* rather than chance. Unfortunately, none of these criteria, either singly or in conjunction with the others, demonstrates how creative thinking might be different from other kinds of thought.

Creativeness and Quality

In his book *Artistry: The Work of Artists*, Vernon A. Howard (1982) asserts that "to create is not only to do, but to do well" (p. 126). David N. Perkins (1981), in another volume with an indicative title, *The Mind's Best Work*, says "creative means original and of high quality" (p. 6). In these two quotations the authors are obviously not talking about people at all, but about how words are used—or should be used— according to the authors' points of view. They have decided in advance to call nothing creative that does not meet their exacting standards. When they discuss creating and creativeness, they are not talking about activities, or attitudes, or even vocations, but about performance. Two individuals may be applying paint to canvas or carving stone, but whether or not they are being creative would depend on how favorably their efforts are evaluated. It is like saying that people are not capable of running, jumping, or swimming unless they can break records, or at least reach prescribed standards of performance.

But if quality is a criterion, then statements about the creativeness of individuals become arbitrary and relative. They become statements about style and fashion, rather than about anything a person might be capable of doing. What is valued at one time may not be valued at another. Van Gogh and Schubert were ignored or deplored for most of their lifetimes, their work regarded as worthless, and they themselves considered devoid of talent. Yet later (often too late for the individuals concerned) a change in fashion, convention, or critical opinion may suddenly elevate the status of artists and their work. The artists and their products have not changed, but taste and fashion have.

Notions of "quality" and "value" change even faster and more unpredictably these days with the commercialization of art. Names become more important than products. Must we say that the more valued person is more creative?

Nevertheless, the attitude that "creativeness" must imply high quality is common. An unknown painter may do everything that a more successful (or more fashionable) painter does, but be denied the status of a creative individual. By the "high-standard" criterion, creativeness is not a characteristic of the person but a reflection of the attitudes of the time. People can be accorded, or denied, creativeness retroactively.

Originality

Originality presents as many problems as a mark of creativeness as quality. The word *original* is itself ambiguous; it can mean that something is done that has never been done before, or simply that something is done without the knowledge that it has been done before. If absolute priority is demanded, then an idea can be creative only for the person who has it first. (Claiming originality is nevertheless an important practical consideration, as shown by the concern that inventors have with patents and scientists with priority in publication.) On the other hand, requiring that a person should not know that someone else has done something first almost makes ignorance a requirement for a creative act.

Creative thinking occurs despite the fact that someone has done the same thing before. "Reinventing the wheel" is not necessarily a waste of time, if a subsequent creator gains a deeper understanding, or if an earlier solution is independently verified. Starting anew may involve less time and effort than searching for an existing solution, in the same way that it is more practical for a library to buy a new copy of a book than to search for one lost in the stacks.

There are many ways to be creative without being innovative. Not all painting, composing, dancing, or writing is unique, but they nevertheless make possible experience that would not otherwise exist. If priority is a criterion, then creativeness becomes a matter of chance. If you are first, you are creative; if not, you are out of luck. This is absurd. Originality, like quality, says nothing about what a person actually does, only about the circumstances in which it is done. It does not enlighten us about the nature of the person or the thought behind the act.

Intention

I have just said that creativeness judged in terms of quality and originality becomes a matter of chance—depending on current fashion and whether someone else had done the same thing. Yet in a different context chance is the one thing that is not permitted in creativeness. There must be intention. Artists are expected to *work* for their results (even when they intentionally allow chance to be a factor). There is no credit for art that might have occurred by chance alone—that is why nature, animals, and infants can never be artistic, no matter how aesthetically pleasing their products might happen to be.

In fact, chance is a crucial component of every creative enterprise. Painters often do not know what kind of brushstroke, what shade of color, what balance of forms will give them the effect they want. They proceed by experimentation, by trial and error, exploring whether a desired consequence can by chance be attained. Composers extemporize to discover a harmony they seek. Authors put characters on paper and wait for their story to emerge. There is a great deal of "found art" in all art, the artistry lying not so much in the generation of possibilities, which is often left to a kind of guided happenstance, as in the selection of the most appropriate possibility. Art is not always intentional.

In other words, the third criterion for creativeness must fail, not only in explaining creative thinking or creative behavior, but in accounting for how the word *creative* is generally used. These criteria are themselves examples of creative thinking, aimed at defining how the term should be used.

Who Is Called Creative?

Despite all the efforts to achieve definition, not much attention is paid to the criteria of high quality, originality, or effort when people are in fact credited with being "creative." The term is usually attributed on the basis of how people typically spend their time, by occupation rather than by achievement. Almost by definition, people who are employed in the "arts," or who make a living out of them, are characterized as creative. Once again, this tells us nothing about what creativeness might actually be—except that creative people are often expected to produce "artistic" products.

Some people may be called creative even when they do not conspicuously produce work of high quality and originality, provided they are in the right occupation. Individuals associated with music, drama, literature, poetry, dance, or design are likely to be considered creative, no matter how limited the imagination they demonstrate. They are distinguished by the fact that they participate in the creation of new experience for other people. Their creativeness is not open to doubt. They make the world a different place for the rest of us.

For individuals not in one of the "artistic" occupations, however, the criteria for creativeness become a little more relevant. Something out of the ordinary, or at least of high quality, has to be achieved by people in "crafts" such as ceramics or weaving, or in technologies such as photography and computer programming, to receive the accolade of creativeness. Scientists and engineers can be called creative if they are sufficiently ingenious and inventive. Creativeness can be associated with the business world, especially among entrepreneurs. Gardeners and cooks can be creative, and so can accountants (although for them the term is not necessarily complimentary). Creativeness can be a matter of style—creative people do unexpected things, in their dress, their furnishings, and their behavior. Individuals can be creative in committees, even in bureaucracies.

The word *art* itself has a wide range of meanings. It has a general sense, which includes literature and music, and a specific sense, which excludes them. Art museums and galleries can be relied on to display paintings and sculpture but not books and music. In the previous chapter, I was concerned with art in the limited sense of painting and sculpture, in contrast to literature and music. In the present chapter I am concerned with art more generally, including literature and music.

The words *art* and *literature* are used in inconsistent ways. "Children's art" is usually done by children. No one claims that it is up to the standards of adult art—age is taken into account—and it is not expected to have the same motivation (though it may in fact better demonstrate the urge to create new realities). "Children's literature," on the other hand, is usually written by adults, although it is not necessarily literature in terms of the high-quality criterion applied to people who write *for* adults. (The word *adult* has itself acquired an interesting connotation in the commercially creative world of books and movies, where it is adjectivally synonymous with *erotic*.) But while the word *literature* may be denied to most of the authors whose works appear in bookstores, it is used indiscriminately as a generic term for assorted printed materials—such as instructional manuals, advertising brochures, or political tracts. In the same way, many painters are denied the distinction of producing art, although the term is extensively used for anything graphic (*art-work*) that is printed on paper. Artists with the qualification "commercial" before their name are not awarded the status of those who are "pure" artists, although the latter are not necessarily less interested in making a living.

Despite the multiple meanings of words like art, creative, and creativity, they are usually comprehensible in the context in which they are used. But they do not describe anything more than what people can be seen doing, or say they do. The words do not explain how people are able to do such things. They tell us what is going on in the world, not in the human brain.

There is a risk of believing that people have to *have* creativity in order to be creative. Creativity becomes an explanation in itself. But the word tells us nothing about people's minds. Perkins (1981) says that having creativity does not explain creative behavior any more than having "athleticity" would explain athletic achievement.

To talk of creativeness, on the other hand, is to describe how people behave. Creative people *create*—that is the point. They do not think about creating, they do not talk about it; they do it. This is the reason I have been employing the slightly awkward term *creativeness* rather than the more familiar word *creativity* in talking about creative people. I have also preferred to avoid the term *creative thinking*, with its implication of a special kind of thinking, in favor of *thinking creatively*, which suggests thinking in a particular way, a style or manner rather than a distinctive process. Thinking creatively is like thinking constructively, aggressively, sympathetically, pessimistically, or sardonically—not a different kind of thinking, but a manner of thinking on particular occasions.

So what are people saying when they argue about the nature of creative thought and creativity, and the need to have more of them? They are often not talking about the creativeness of people, or what creative people do, but about the use of words. They are constructing a conceptual framework that does not necessarily correspond to the reality of how people are in fact creative. People who are creative do not necessarily create in ways that meet ephemeral criteria of high quality or originality, nor do they necessarily do so deliberately. Creative people do something else. They create worlds of experience that can be shared, which might otherwise not exist. They demonstrate creativeness the way they might demonstrate eagerness or sincerity, by the way in which they do things.

People who are concerned about creative thinking, and who want it taught in schools, are usually not talking about *creativeness*, the propensity of the brain to create, nor indeed about the creative nature of thought, which remains concealed in the mind, but about what people demonstrate when they *create*, when they produce something that other people can experience and examine. This concern may be well founded, because few of us create as much as we could or as well as we could, but not because we lack creativity skills.

THE EXPERIENCE OF ART

What is entailed in *thinking creatively?* I have been talking only about words so far, and cataloging how a term is used does not reveal what is going on in the brain. But at least it discloses what people seem to be talking about. And it seems as if people are talking about two things when they talk about creative thinking. In general, the reference is to the creation of art, especially art that is considered to be novel and of high quality. But in addition, perhaps by analogy, the term may be used for any thinking that is novel and highly regarded, particularly "solutions" to problems. So if we are to explore what people do when they are credited with creativeness (or what they lack if they are not), we might best begin by considering art and looking at what makes it valued (apart from vogue and commercialization). Then we can see whether it is possible to think and act creatively without necessarily producing art of high quality; in other words, whether thinking creatively is more commonplace than it is often taken to be.

We must examine not only how art is produced, but why. What do artists get out of producing works of art, and what does art do for people who may not produce it, but simply "enjoy" it? Why do people bring art into their homes, and seek it in libraries, art galleries, and concert halls? Why do they sometimes fight for its expression in law courts?

I shall begin by discussing the appeal of art to those who have not produced it themselves. There is no convenient term for such people— for the consumers (ugly word), patrons (sexist), audience (limited), participants (ambiguous), recipients (awkward), art lovers (florid), or the public (bureaucratic). I must resort to circumlocutions, like *experienc-*

ing art, and occasionally employ the words *participant* or *audience* in a very broad sense.

Sensitivity to Art

Simply put, art in all its various manifestations provides opportunities for experience that would not otherwise exist, for experiences that may be particularly heightened, desirable, and unusual, but not for experiences involving thoughts and feelings different in character from those we might have in other situations. There can be no such experiences. We respond to art the way we respond to the rest of the world. We may have heightened sensitivities to some forms of art, but we can have the same heightened sensitivities to aspects of the world in general. There are no specialized sense organs for art. There is nothing unique about what people do to enjoy or produce art. There is frequently something unique about *artists*, however, not because they have different kinds of brains, but because of the different kinds of things they create. As a result, we may regard artists with respect, admiration, and even awe.

Art extends the world. Art can be accessible through any of the sensory systems by which we experience the physical world, and we respond to art in the ways we respond to that world, with the same kind of thoughts and the same kind of feelings. Special knowledge may be needed about art in order to enjoy and understand it, to experience it fully, but special knowledge is required to experience fully other aspects of the world. The fact that special knowledge is required to experience something does not mean that something is experienced in a unique way.

Some people may have more "artistic sensitivity" than others, but that simply means a greater propensity to *respond* to art, even to seek it out. It means being particularly aware of art, in the way that other people might be particularly aware of the weather, or of birdsong, or of fashion. Artistic sensitivity is a *disposition*, a readiness to experience art, a different interest and focus of attention, but not a different kind of awareness or attention. All thinking involves sensitivities.

Art extends our lives. Encounters with art are driven by the same impulses that compel us to find experience in reality—the need to create and explore meaningful worlds. The appeal of art is the appeal of life. We respond to art in the same way we respond to the objective world. We respond with *feelings*—of happiness or sadness, acceptance or rejection, inspiration or discouragement, enlightenment or confusion.

There is art for all the senses—paintings and plays to be seen, novels and poetry to be read, music to be heard (and danced to), dance to be experienced visually and kinesthetically. Artistic experiences in smell, taste, and touch are limited by technology—but they are being explored, and there is an aesthetic for all of them. Not only can the new worlds of art be presented to all the sensory systems, they engage all the "senses" behind them—our sense of what is fit, relevant, appropriate, ridiculous. In other words, all our thought can be engaged, and all of our feelings behind our thought. Everything the world can do to our thoughts and feelings, art can do.

We use the same language to talk about the arts that we use for real-world experience, except when using purely technical terms, and even then there is a great deal of borrowing for metaphorical use. We talk of the *perspective* of authors (in their *visualizations* of character), the *harmonies* of painters (in particular *passages* of their works), and the *drama* of musical scores (in *dialogs* between instruments). We talk of being moved or excited by a work's appeal, and our involvement with it; we talk of our preferences, understandings, and confusions. Art is no different from life.

We can lose our way in a novel, a painting, or a symphony just as we can lose our way in an unfamiliar city. We may lose patience if we are not prepared to slow down and accustom ourselves to new surroundings. All artists have their own conventions, their own symbols and metaphors, which we must respect if we are to experience their creations in any depth. But this again is just like life; we have to respect the fact that all human behavior is conventional.

Dress, ornamentation, home decoration, cars, architecture—all are conventional. There are conventional ways to be unconventional. If we are completely unconventional, we are misunderstood. Novelty does not mean unconventionality, but rather fitting into convention in new or unexpected ways. Art is typically conventional, or unconventional in conventional ways. Where art of any kind departs too radically from convention, there is debate about whether it should be given or denied the title of *art*.

The essential qualities of great art—of the novels, poems, sculptures, paintings, symphonies, and songs that have come to us through the ages—are the intensity and value of the experiences they make possible. Art is valued if it generates deep or new or lasting patterns of thought and feeling. It may also *tell* us things, but it does not have to, any more than the world has to tell us things. But it must stimulate powerful thoughts and feelings.

Of course, value is relative, and so are judgments of art. That is why there can be no clear definition of what constitutes a work of art at any time. In fact art itself is a relatively modern invention. In their time, Leonardo and Michelangelo were considered craftsmen. Much of what is seen as art today was not created to be art; for example, the contents of the tombs of Egyptian and Chinese rulers that are so prominent in contemporary museums. For art to be popularly valued, it has to be done at the right time, in the right places, and in the right way— "right" in each case meaning conventional. Luck is also involved; luck for the artist to be in the right place at the right time with an acceptable product, and also on occasion the luck to be marketed in a resourceful manner.

Why Sensitivity Fails

Why are some people insensitive to art—or rather, why are most of us insensitive to some kinds of art? The reasons must be the same—and as complex—as the reasons we all are disinclined to engage in certain aspects of life. If people do not universally engage in art, it is not because they lack an ability to think creatively or to think "artistically."

Failure to understand a poem or painting or symphony can be as perplexing and frustrating as an incomprehensible aspect of the real world—a complex piece of machinery, perhaps, or the impenetrable workings of a quartz clock, an electronic toy, or a computer. Complexity without comprehension induces boredom, irritation, and anxiety.

People become accustomed to perceiving the world in a particular way. Intolerance of differences—in art, in other people, even in food and dress—results in disinterest, rejection, fear, and contempt. "Incomprehensible" art can provoke hostility because it threatens the stories we have so carefully constructed about how the world makes sense. On the other hand, some people doubtless say they enjoy art without truly doing so; art can add a cachet to the character being written for oneself.

Everyone has the potential to enter and experience the worlds of art. No rare abilities are involved, no unique mental skills or states. At one time the world that is now so obvious to us must have been as unfamiliar as the latest experiments in music, literature, and painting. Babies do not make sense of the world because of any intrinsic characteristics it may have; they bring meaning to it. And with this meaning-making exploration comes knowledge, excitement, and satisfaction. Art offers extensions of the experiences we have in the world, provided we can embrace the realities of art the way we embraced the reality of the objective world.

THE CREATION OF ART

Imagination is power. The creativeness of thought that enables us all to experience the world in which we live—and to experience the art that can become part of that world—also makes it possible to construct new realities ourselves, and that is power indeed. Feelings that come with the experience of art can be even more profound in the delights, frustrations, and mysteries of creating art. Creation is the imagination going beyond the constraints of the presented world, beyond the necessities and exigencies of objective reality, producing of our own volition new and different worlds to explore, enjoy, and share. In addition to thinking creatively, we can *create*.

The creation of art is the creation of realities out of *nothing*. Creating is, as the dictionary tells us, to bring into being, to cause to exist, *to form out of nothing*. It is the *realization*—the making real—of the imaginative potential of the brain.[1]

Artists do not need audiences. They may appreciate them at appropriate times, and possibly depend on their support or patronage for psychological or practical reasons, but the first, primary, and often only audience for an artist is the artist. Artists create to express, please, and satisfy themselves (though they are not necessarily the ones most pleased or satisfied by their creations). Artists are the first to explore the worlds they create, and they explore them in ways no one else can, even though others may come to know their books, paintings, and concertos better than they do. (Performers may have a similar but different creative acquaintance with a work of art when they "interpret" a part in a play, a ballet, or a concerto; a performance is a work of creation.) The relationship of artists to their created works is like that of parents to children—they may not know them as well as other people, but they have a more intimate relationship with them.

Artists are *creators*, and art is the realization of worlds that we all have the potential of creating. Every human brain wants to experience and explore; that is a reflection of the creative nature of the brain. But the brain cannot be restricted to experiencing and exploring the worlds that happen to exist, that we happen to encounter. How could the brain be restricted in advance to making sense only of the conditions in which it will find itself?

The brain must be open-ended in its quest to create worlds. Otherwise it could never make sense of the world in which it actually exists. It must be—at the very least—an overflow from this drive to find sense in given worlds that leads the brain to create new worlds of art. Creating is a fundamental and continual urge, and it is a restriction on human potential that so few people do it.

The Act of Creation

At the heart of any work of art is the basic act of pattern-recognition that enables the imagination to impose sense on real or imaginary worlds, a tangible realization that can be seen, heard, or otherwise experienced and shared in some way. The creation of art, in any medium, always involves the two familiar elements of the active imagination: the generation of alternatives and selection among those alternatives.

An artist must be able to create possibilities—the words that convey a desired emotional tone, the colors (or the notes) that contrast with just the right degree of dramatic conflict. It is too much to expect just the right idea at just the right time. Creations do not unravel from the human brain fully formed, even in those remarkable cases when the artist seems capable of putting the entire story on paper, the picture on canvas, or the melody on the keyboard, without hesitation or revision.

We can all create spontaneously, to order, in trivial ways. We write a short note for ourselves, or for a friend, and it comes out right first time. More remarkably, perhaps, most of the time we manage to *say* things that come out right the first time, even though they are almost certainly things we have never said before. But just because the performance is flawless, it does not mean that we did not first examine alternatives in our mind. The performance can be right the first time *because* the alternatives have already been examined and decided upon. Even when only one alternative "fits," when the solution to a problem is uniquely and obviously right, that does not mean that other possibilities have not been sought, examined, and rejected. All thinking is creative.

The more unusual the circumstances, the more complex the problem or ambitious and original the intention, the more important the generation of alternatives becomes. *Divergent thinking* is a popular term in some analyses of problem-solving and creative thinking—the divergence referring to the range of possible solutions that are considered, the alternatives that are generated. But divergent thinking is merely commonplace thinking about a broad range of possibilities, without jumping to premature conclusions. The alternatives that the brain creates are the landscape through which an artist travels, selecting only the fruits that are ripe for harvesting.

When we are intentionally creative—when we sit down to write a poem, or compose a song, or program a computer—we constantly deal with alternatives. Part of the competence of people who are identified as creative is in the range of possibilities they generate. We will usually not be very creative if we can entertain only one possibility in a situation.

The generation of alternatives is the "inspired" part of artistic creation, although it often demands persistence, patience, and confidence. It also demands experience to provide acquaintance with a topic from which rich possibilities can arise; knowledge of the technical requirements for the expression of ideas; and a foundation for the mental resolution to continue the search for possibilities. No one becomes inspired without experience. The range of a painter's ideas expands with familiarity with what others have painted in the past, with painting techniques and materials, and with the frustrations and exhilaration of painting. Experience tells how long to persevere and when to stop.

While the generation of alternatives involves a patient relaxation, a deliberate openness to other possibilities, *selection* requires a different kind of discipline. It demands a ruthless objectivity with one's own creations. Writers, painters, and composers must all *edit*.

Selection among alternatives also improves with experience. Not all artists can generate and select to the same degree. Some may be prolific with their ideas but not have the knowledge or the fortitude to make appropriate choices. They cannot recognize—or admit—that parts of their creations should be modified or excised. Writers are frequently helped by editors who could not themselves generate the alternatives that the author has created, but who can nevertheless help the author to create better. Others can play similarly constructive roles for painters and musicians.

Generation and selection are not stages in an artistic process that take place just once, in that order, for any particular work. Generation and selection are part of a continuous, seamless, creative act. What is done right now is the culmination of everything done up to that point, but the beginning of everything to come. Artistic creation is always an interaction between the artist and the realization. That is the reason it is usually better to start than to do nothing. It is easier to develop or amend something that has begun than something that remains in the mind. Little is written, painted, or composed if there is a reluctance to commit possibilities to paper or canvas.

The Specifications of Artists

How do artists know that they have achieved what they want to achieve, that they should stop? How indeed can anyone say that something is completed that is *novel*, that is not a replica or repetition of anything else? How can an author say, "That is the story I wanted to write," or a composer, "That is the music I wanted to hear"? The answer cannot be that the work is preformed in the creator's head. If it were, there would be no more creating to do. In any case, the question would still have to be answered: How is the work in the creator's head recognized as what the creator wanted to achieve (or, for that matter, not yet what the creator wanted)?

This is an important and very general question, because all creators must have a *guide* to direct the work of creation, from the original intention to the final completed realization. And obviously, this guide must change continually as the creation develops. The guide at the beginning cannot be as detailed and certain as the guide at the end; otherwise the creator would begin with full knowledge of what is to be created. In fact, what *develops* during the creation of a work of art is not so much the work itself as the *idea* of the work in the artist's mind— the guide that keeps the artist on task and confirms when the task is finished.

I have already referred to the ever-developing *specifications* that are constantly in our head, combinations of intentions and expectations, that enable us to make our worlds a meaningful place. Specifications also guide the development of works of art. There is nothing exceptional about the specifications of artists, except for their subject matter. The intentions and expectations we have for creating an understanding of the real world are identical with the specifications we have for creating new realities.

An author's initial specification may be very sketchy—little more than an intention to write a story with a particular central character. At every point in the development of the work, alternatives are explored and selections made—the two aspects of creation—at global and at focal levels. The specification is in effect a developing description of the finished work. At any point the creator might go back and revise the work, and the specification. This is the basis of learning.

And when the realization is congruent with a specification to the author's satisfaction—when the work matches its intended description—then the work is done. By that time the realization will be far more detailed than the specification (there is always more in a book than there ever was at any one time in the author's head). Of course, no specification has only one realization; and a single realization of a specification is not usually the end of the artist's endeavor. New specifications, "new ideas," are created in the process of trying to develop a realization of an original specification.

This is the reason artistic collaborations are rare and difficult. Two or more people rarely get together in writing a novel, painting a picture, or composing a piece of music (unless one is clearly in charge and the others are assistants). *Realization* is too idiosyncratic, too personal. Each step along the way is interpreted differently by each collaborator; they are living through different experiences. It is not a question of deciding what should be done next, but of agreeing on where they are up to that point. They are working from different specifications. Where teams of people try to collaborate, on movies, ballets, and operas, there can be serious conflicts.

Specifications direct and control behavior (even while the consequences of behavior redirect the shape and texture of specifications). The skill of an artist lies in the ability to create and execute specifications that result in realizations that meet the artist's demands and expectations—and, if the artist is concerned with a public response, with the demands and expectations of others.

Achieving Creativeness

No matter how independent and solitary many artists might seem, creativeness—in any form—must have its roots in experience, mostly in experience gained with other people. Experience has to teach three things: what can be done through art (or any other creative enterprise), how these things are done, and that these things are open for anyone to do. No one is born with any of this knowledge.

If you are to be a writer you must know that books and stories (or plays or poems) exist. You must know that people *write* stories (and other kinds of books), that writing is a human activity. None of this knowledge can be inherited, or be a biological predisposition. People who become writers must learn, through experience, that a world of writing exists—and they cannot learn this by themselves.

No one ever, at one fell swoop, invented the idea of stories, the idea of writing, and the idea of becoming a writer, establishing and making use of all the necessary conventions and technology. No one individual could devise such a complex cultural phenomenon, so much of which depends on personal interaction and collaboration. No one person ever invented music, or painting, nor is it possible for anyone today to reinvent music or painting, starting from nothing. The worlds of music and painting, like the world of writing, can only be discovered through experience. The first requirement for becoming an artist is the discovery that other people engage in artistic activities—that there are "clubs" of writers, painters, and musicians that can be joined.

Libraries, museums, theaters, concert halls, radio, television, and other technology can all contribute to extending knowledge about literature, painting, and music—but the beginning of this knowledge, the getting started, must depend on experience with other people who are already engaged in the activity. They show what is possible, both in experiencing art and in producing it.

But the people who provide continuing support, and the basis for extended learning, do not have to be personal acquaintances. They are the *practitioners* who write the books, paint the pictures, and compose and perform the music and dance that furnish the worlds of the various artistic clubs. These people may not be immediately accessible—in fact, they can be dead—but they teach by what they have created. You can learn by reading what they have done, seeing or hearing what they have done (or by reading about what they have done). They show what can be done and the conventions observed in doing it.

There remains one thing that no amount of experience with artistic products can provide, which is the second requirement for artistic creativeness—the mastery of mediums, of tools, materials, and techniques. A painting does not reveal how the painter mixed paints or wiped brushes, and a novel does not show the use of paper clips and index cards, or editing. No finished product in any medium shows the false starts that went into it, the trial and error, the frustration and exhilaration. This is knowledge that initially must come from others, through participatory experience. There is still room for personal inventiveness, but every innovator has to have a point from which to start.

Finally, all artists have to learn that they can do artistic things themselves. We are not aware of the powers we are born with, and potential does not naturally develop into potency. Dispositions must be brought under at least a degree of focused control. Persistence (without compulsiveness), commitment, confidence, patience, and tolerance for uncertainty and ambiguity may all be individual personality characteristics, but they all have to be shaped and controlled so that they are constructive, and all this can only be learned through experience.[2]

I have not talked of talent, because I am arguing that everyone can be an artist. Everyone thinks creatively. Artists may be special people, not because they have different kinds of brains, but because of the different kinds of thing they accomplish. I am not arguing that everyone can be a virtuoso. In every activity some people will do very much better than others. Unless there is an obvious physical handicap, we can all run, in our own fashion, even if few of us will reach Olympic standards. We do not normally bewail our inability to achieve world records, or complain that we were born without running ability, unless we put ourselves into competition with outstanding athletes.

We belittle our own artistic talent and that of others, not because of what we are capable of achieving but because of the comparisons we make with what others can do. It is ironic that in matters of art, which can be of such great personal satisfaction (and where public acclaim is so arbitrary and unpredictable), we tend to draw such invidious comparisons with the public performances of others (and with the transient tastes of commercialization and fashion).

"Natural talent" is woven from many threads. No *specific* inborn characteristic can account for great artists. Piano playing cannot be in the genes, nor can painting or writing. The technologies are too recent to have been genetically established.

A "natural" musician must have a developed sense of many things related to the rhythms and harmonies of music, together with a number of general physical characteristics—endurance, dexterity, and eye-hand coordination—and many psychological factors, like persistence, determination, and a variety of blends of "sensitivities." There are so many factors in every art that less than optimum abilities in one area can sometimes be compensated for by superiority in others. In a performing musician, for example, exceptional dexterity may compensate for small hands; a driving energy may counterbalance lack of early experience.

It is not only specially gifted and dedicated people who are creative. Everybody, all the time, thinks as creatively as artists think—they just think creatively about different things. If you do not think about artistic matters, or undertake artistic endeavors, you will not be thinking "artistically," although you may still be thinking creatively. The exclusive thing about artistic activity is its outcome—and even then the difference depends on what happens to be called *art*.

Every moment of every day the brain is engaged in the imaginative generation and selection of alternative possibilities that are the basis of art. It is not called *art*, not because it lacks creativeness, but because it does not have the arbitrary characteristics of art that I have discussed—a perceived value, novelty, and evident intention. Commonplace creative thinking is not called *art*, simply because it is not engaged in for artistic purposes and is not viewed in artistic ways.

The brain is creative when we imagine a conversation we might have or wish we had had; we are doing what a playwright does. It is creative when we fantasize the setting of an important meeting; we are doing what a film director does.

Everyone is creative; we all have the potential for creating. But commonplace creativity is not particularly valued, because there is no scarcity of it. Commonplace thinking appears unoriginal, but only because it is taken for granted. We all have to create the world for ourselves; we cannot copy anyone else's image.

Why Creativeness Fails

Why do some people think more creatively than others? (Or rather, why do all of us fail to act as creatively as we might on some occasions?) "Lack of creativity" explains nothing; everyone has the potential to be creative. Poor *performance* in creative matters may be due to lack of skills and knowledge in a particular medium, but not to lack of "creativeness skills."

I am unlikely to be creative in painting or music because I do not know enough about painting or music. I am not familiar with the conventions and with the history. Paintings, symphonies, and novels cannot be "made up"; there is a need to know how they are constructed, just as there is a need to know about the equipment and materials involved in their creation. Creativeness is not a skill, but skills are involved in expressing creativeness. You do not learn to be creative by creativeness exercises, but you learn to capitalize on creativeness through mastery of a medium. We cannot create a world of physics if we know nothing of physics, nor an imaginary conversation if our experience of conversations is limited. Creativeness necessarily fails when its expression is thwarted by ignorance, inexperience, or feebleness of intention.

If we can respond to our surroundings at all, we are all born able to enjoy singing, dancing, building castles out of sand, pictures out of colors, and anything else that other people show us are enjoyable and possible. As children there was probably a time when we all sang, danced, and made pictures of great imagination. What stops us is not a lack of ability or desire, but *concern with results*. We become worried about what other people will think of us if they see us engaging in the activity. Many adults will not paint because they feel they have nothing to say; they are reluctant to sing or dance because they are afraid they will be ridiculed. Creative expression does not die because it becomes meaningless to us but because other people want to put relative values upon it.[3]

Technology and Creativeness

Computers have created no new arts; art produced on computers— or with the aid of computers—appeals to the same feelings that are inspired by other forms of art and by the world. The creative thought that has always gone into writing, painting, and music has now been extended into computers. Computers augment possibilities for creativeness.

Computers have not made other forms of art outdated, any more than they have made earlier tools, techniques, and materials obsolescent. They are a new kind of writing machine for authors, a new kind of brush for painters, a new kind of instrument for musicians. The computer screen is a different material for artists to work on. Computers have helped artists create new worlds of animation, of simulations and games, new kinds of maps, new kinds of models, new kinds of landscapes.

Computers can help everyone who wants to become more creative. They offer the wonderful advantage of being fast and efficient in doing many of the things we all want or have to do—creating arrays of words, numbers or images, modifying, elaborating, organizing, storing, and recovering them.

Some people fear that computers make things too easy. It is argued that children will never learn to spell if computers are always available to check spellings and supply correct ones; that no one will want to draw if computers can make perfect circles and straight lines; and that there is something degenerate if not immoral in colors that do not run, that can be erased and replaced at a whim. These objections come from people who seem to think that nothing is worth doing unless it is difficult, and that learning and thinking are moved forward by obstacles rather than facilitation.

Computers and other technology cannot inhibit creative thought or learning, unless we are inhibited by technology in the first place. Technology does not suppress the imagination unless we allow it to.

To recapitulate, the word *creative* is used selectively and misleadingly with respect to thought. The term is usually limited to the context of certain kinds of activity that achieve arbitrary standards of quality and originality. The word *art* is even more restricted in its use and is inconsistent in its designation. But people can be creative without being artistic, and we all think creatively, whether or not we engage in activities that are called *creative* and *artistic*. To become conspicuous as creative thinkers, people need experience and encouragement in creative and artistic activities, not special training in general "creative thinking skills." Precisely the same considerations apply to *critical* thinking.

7

THINKING CRITICALLY

Creative thinking and critical thinking are usually treated as distinct topics, with entire books devoted to one or the other. When there are complaints that too many people are incapable of thinking creatively, or of thinking critically, it is not usually considered that these might be the same thing.

But is the brain doing something different in "thinking creatively" and "thinking critically"? Is either a distinct mental process or a unique collection of skills? In the previous chapter I proposed that there was nothing exceptional about thinking creatively. In the present chapter, I shall examine whether "critical" thought is any different from "creative" thought, except for the circumstances in which they take place.

Much of the debate and uncertainty about critical thinking again concerns language, and there are frequent disputations about "what critical thinking really is." Nevertheless the term is widely used, especially in education, to refer to mental activity that is supposed to be special and even uncommon. That is the reason I have given the topic a chapter to itself in this book. The discussion will begin with some critical thought about what lies behind all the discussions of critical thinking.

TALKING ABOUT CRITICAL THINKING

There is a big difference between the way critical thinking is discussed in the world in general and in the narrower world of education. In fact, critical thinking is rarely discussed in the world at large; it is not a common expression on anyone's tongue. I have yet to hear people wish they could be better critical thinkers, or ask for a little less noise because they are trying to think critically, the way they might say they are trying to read or watch television. Deploring the ability of other people to think is an ancient and popular pastime, especially with reference to students, subordinates, or a younger generation, but such complaints are usually related to thought generally, to ill-defined generalities like "intelligence" or "smartness," not to anything as specific as "critical thinking." When critical aspects of thought are mentioned, it is usually with reference to personality characteristics, to habitual or customary attitudes, rather than to a particular skill—and not necessarily to a socially desirable way of behaving.

In education, however, concern with something specific called *critical thinking* has reached almost obsessive proportions. Statements of educational objectives, particularly in social studies and English, often refer to a need for more and better critical thought. Critical thinking is perceived as a valuable skill, or set of skills, lacking in large numbers of students from grade school to university. It is assumed that the skills can be learned, and therefore taught, and also measured in objective tests. But oddly enough, while the term is so assertively employed, there is great uncertainty about what it actually means, especially among people who are motivated to "improve education" or who are held responsible for the improvement.

While the world in general tends to regard the way people think in terms of their motives, personality characteristics, or general competence, educators typically perceive thinking in terms of skills and deficiencies, of learning and teaching. If students do not behave in a certain manner, it is assumed that they are unable to do so, not that they might prefer not to.

Definitions and Descriptions

An educational journal article whose title asks the blunt question, "Critical Thinking: What Is It?," begins:

> Answering this question is not as easy as one might expect—or hope—it would be. If most educators do not seem to agree about one thing, it is the nature of this important thinking skill. Yet developing an accurate, commonly accepted definition of critical thinking is absolutely essential. Until we can develop such a definition, teachers, curriculum builders, and instructional materials and test developers will be unable to help all youngsters learn this skill as well as they might (Beyer, 1985, p. 270).

I have not singled out Professor Beyer's paper because it is exceptionally flawed, but because it demonstrates in a conveniently compact manner presuppositions that are typically made about "critical thinking." The article also displays a widespread academic faith in the power of definitions. The author wants a definition, not a description, of critical thinking. His opening paragraph explicitly states (1) that critical thinking is an "important thinking skill" (even though most educators do not agree on its nature) and (2) that not all youngsters will learn to think critically as well as they might until a commonly accepted and "accurate" definition of the term is developed, at which time (3) teachers, curriculum builders, and instructional materials and test developers will be able to help everyone to become critical thinkers.

But Beyer's opening remarks are about the use of words in the language, not about a skill. (Only words can be defined; skills, behavior, and attitudes must be described.) A better title for the article might have been "Critical Thinking: What Are People Talking About?" And it is clearly not correct that we have to wait for a commonly accepted definition of critical thinking before everyone can learn to engage in it. Some people—including, presumably, authorities on the topic—must already be regarded as capable of critical thinking, despite the absence of a commonly accepted definition. And given that there is so little agreement about the nature of critical thinking and how it should be defined, an enormous leap of faith is required for the belief that it can be taught through curriculums, instructional materials, and tests. Perhaps a quite different approach might be required, employing example rather than instruction, encouragement rather than materials, and opportunities rather than tests.

Defining a word cannot throw any light on the nature of its referent—a definition reflects how words are used, not whatever reality there might be behind the words. (The dictionary's own definition of *definition* as "a precise statement of the essential nature of a thing" exemplifies how unrealistic definitions can be; any insight a definition gives into the nature of a thing is incidental at best.) In any case—to return to Beyer—it is difficult to see how an "accurate" definition of *critical thinking* might be achieved. Would it involve an analysis of how people behave, or how they talk? What would the yardstick be? Who would decide that accuracy had been achieved? And how would such a definition be "commonly accepted"? Language use is not determined by fiat, or even by deliberate consensus.

Beyer goes on to say that "Specialists today appear to agree that . . . critical thinking is the assessing of the authenticity, accuracy and/or worth of knowledge claims and arguments" (1985, p. 271). (A specialist might be defined as someone who speaks with authority with whom we do not disagree.) But are Beyer's specialists describing what people who engage in critical thinking do (a kind of job description) or are they also merely describing how the term is used (or should be used)?

Such specialists have already made up their mind that something called *critical thinking* exists. They talk about it as something uncommon yet distinctive, like a rare bird that they have been able to identify. They do not talk about critical (or creative) aspects of commonplace thinking, which presumably can be neither creative nor critical.

Despite the fact that Beyer begins by alluding to the semantic uncertainty surrounding critical thinking, he proceeds immediately to his own conclusion that it is a skill (although later in his article he frequently refers to it as a *set* of skills). But is critical thinking a skill? Is that the best way to regard it?

The word *skills* is used very loosely in education, often in circumstances where *knowledge* might be more appropriate. What are called *library skills*, for example, involve knowing how books are organized on shelves and references on files. Library skills are not physical activities like typewriting, running, or jumping, where practice and instruction can result in the development of muscular coordination and strength—and neither is thinking. No muscles are involved in thinking. Krashen (1984) observes that the development of so-called language skills depends on understanding rather than practice, and the same might be said about thinking (see also Note 2, Chapter 1).

I have headed this chapter "Thinking Critically" rather than "Critical Thinking"—as I headed the previous chapter "Thinking Creatively"—to try to avoid the immediate assumption that there are exclusive and alternative modes of thought, called *critical* and *creative*, that involve distinct mental functions.

Innumerable qualifiers can be attached to the word *thinking*, apart from *creatively* and *critically*. It is possible to think aggressively, analytically, artistically, boldly, carelessly, charitably, cheerfully, compulsively, constructively, crassly, earnestly, energetically, erratically, fearlessly, flippantly, imaginatively, impulsively, objectively, rationally, reflectively, selfishly, sensitively, seriously, somberly, or suspiciously, to name just a few of the terms that come to mind as I think discursively (or should I say laterally or divergently?). To suggest that just one or two of these appearances of thinking require special status as complex skills or unique mental functions would be arbitrary and invidious, but to give such a unique status to all of them would be absurd.

In everyday language the qualifying terms simply refer to the manner in which thinking is done—to an intention or a disposition, not a distinct mental skill. It is unnecessary to regard "thinking critically" or "thinking creatively," and all the other possibilities, as different *kinds* of thinking. A person's thinking could not be *made* more critical by specific training, any more than exercises could make it more charitable or less flippant. What is required is not more skill, but a change in the person.

ASPECTS OF CRITICAL THINKING

A consequence of calling something as broad as thinking critically a skill is that instructional specialists immediately want to break it down into small parts, which are then referred to as component skills, sub-skills, procedures, or "operations." This is not difficult to do, since it involves nothing more complicated than making up lists, or inventories, of different words that seem to be related to the major topic. The thesaurus is a great resource in such enterprises—I used it myself to construct the list of thinking words at the beginning of this book. But there is no reason to assume that arbitrary lists constitute recipes for thinking critically (or creatively). The items on a list are not ingredients, to be mixed in appropriate quantities and brought to the right degree of heat, in order for the dough of critical thinking to rise.

An astonishing plethora of words is available for the construction of such lists. Distributed throughout Beyer's article, in his own analyses and those that he quotes, are the following forty terms for operations or components of critical thinking:

acting upon	discriminating	questioning
analyzing	distinguishing	recognizing
assessing	drawing (conclusions)	refraining (from
checking	evaluating	jumping to
clarifying	examining	conclusions)
classifying	executing	searching
comparing	extrapolating	seeking
conceptualizing	finding	separating
concluding	grasping	being skeptical
critiquing	identifying	solving
deducing	interpreting	spotting (faults)
detecting	judging	stating
determining	matching	verifying
differentiating	predicting	weighing (evidence)

Of course, some of these terms might be regarded as synonyms, but only on particular occasions. Different specialists could easily reduce the list to different sets of fundamental or underlying processes and skills—but what would be the point? How would we decide who is right? Beyer relies on any consensus that he finds convincing.

Also scattered throughout Beyer's article are sixty-four terms for matters with which critical thought might be concerned:

accuracy	experience	procedures
ambiguity	facts	proof
arguments	fallacies	reasoning
assumptions	generalizations	reasons
authenticity	hypotheses	relationships
authority	inconsistency	relevance
bias	inferences	reliability
claims	information	results
clichés	inventories	rules
clues	judgments	similarities
communication	knowledge	solutions
conclusions	logic	standards
consistency	materials	statements
contradictions	motives	stereotypes
criteria	norms	strategies
data	observations	techniques
deductions	operations	theory
definitions	opinions	validity
differences	overgeneralizations	values
emotions	patterns	worth
equivocation	principles	
evidence	problems	

If the forty components or operations are multiplied by the sixty-four kinds of concern, we come up with 2,560 possibilities for ways in which critical thought might operate. Many of these combinations might be unlikely, redundant, or meaningless, of course—but on what basis would decisions be made to determine whether a particular term makes sense and whether it refers to a specific skill or psychological process?

Nevertheless, in one page of the article I have cited, Beyer sets out eight different lists that he has found of "critical thinking skills" compiled by various specialists, comprising a total of sixty items. The items range from distinguishing between verifiable and unverifiable data and detecting inconsistencies to determining whether an observation statement is reliable and recognizing biased statements.

One of the lists cited by Beyer is from an article by Ennis (1962), which Beyer commends as "probably the most thorough analysis of critical thinking." Ennis's list comprises a dozen components of critical thinking:

1. Grasping the meaning of a statement
2. Judging whether there is ambiguity in a line of reasoning
3. Judging whether certain statements contradict each other
4. Judging whether a conclusion necessarily follows
5. Judging whether a statement is specific enough
6. Judging whether a statement is actually the application of a certain principle
7. Judging whether an observation statement is reliable
8. Judging whether an inductive conclusion is warranted
9. Judging whether the problem has been identified
10. Judging whether something is an assumption
11. Judging whether a definition is adequate
12. Judging whether a statement made by an alleged authority is acceptable

None of the above "skills" is generalizable in any sense. Their application on any particular occasion depends on the specific subject matter that is involved. How can you teach someone to grasp the meaning of a statement (item 1), or to judge whether certain statements contradict each other (item 3), without referring to specific examples? How could someone learn to detect conflicting assertions in a chemistry text, an article on chess, or the estimate for repairs to an automobile, without an understanding of chemistry, chess, or automobile mechanics, in which case contradictions would be immediately apparent? All the items on Ennis's list depend on the first—grasping the meaning of a statement. If there are general rules for grasping the meanings of statements, which some people lack, how could they grasp the meaning of the rules? What must you, the reader, do in order to grasp the meaning of the statements I am making now? Are there rules I could give you that would help? But if you can grasp the meaning of statements, that means that all the other items on Ennis's list follow. If you really grasp the meaning of two statements, and the statements are contradictory, then you would immediately know they are contradictory. If you did not, is there a skill of "detecting contradictions" that could solve your problem for you?

Once again, I am not picking on a particular author because I think he is egregiously wrong. Ennis's list is a useful catalog of things to think about. And it is certainly not unique. But it is also not a list of generalizable skills, and you could not train someone to think critically by teaching them to do all of the things on the list, separately or together, randomly or in any particular order.

Facts and Opinions

As an illustration of the kinds of problems that underlie attempts to create useful lists of critical thinking skills, let me take one almost universal component of such lists, namely, the ability to distinguish between statements of fact and statements of opinion.

Such an ability is something everyone would regard as desirable, in themselves as well as in others. Many people spend large parts of their lives observing the pronouncements of politicians, administrators, advertisers, book reviewers, educational experts, friends, and relatives—and trying to work out if the pronouncements are facts or opinions. The fact (or is it an opinion?) that these observers are often unable to make this distinction surely does not mean that they all lack a fundamental skill. The problem is that they do not have the necessary knowledge—or that they are wrong or biased themselves. There is no formula for distinguishing fact from opinion, no litmus test of veracity, even for our own ideas, let alone those of others. Everything depends on our knowledge (and on whether that knowledge is fact or opinion, an endless regression).

Distinguishing fact from opinion is not a generalizable skill. If someone tells me that Paris is the capital of France and the most beautiful city in Europe, I know the first statement is a fact and the second an opinion, not because of anything particularly skillful that I do, nor because of anything about the way the statements are made, but because of what I know about the world and the way people talk about it.

Opinions may parade as facts, and so might unintentional errors and deliberate lies, but since no statements are marked for any of these characteristics, there is no way we can distinguish them short of knowledge (or opinions) of our own about the subject of the particular statement, about the person making the statement, and the circumstances in which the statement is made. Taking a course in logic or critical thinking will not help anyone detect whether a politician is stretching the truth, though studying the topic the politician is talking about might.

In everyday language and specific circumstances, everyone understands what people mean when they talk about fact and opinion, about knowledge and beliefs. But it is impossible to say what the essential difference *is* between knowledge, beliefs, opinions, assumptions, presuppositions, conjectures, and speculations—matters that confound philosophers, linguists, psychologists, and other experts—because the question is not really answerable. Words do not have specific meanings, though their meaning on any particular occasion usually becomes clear in context. The words *know* and *believe* do not refer to any different ways of thinking, and definitions tell us nothing about their "essences" or about how to distinguish them. If I say I *know* something to be the case, and you then persuade me that my knowledge is really only a belief, I do not shift it to a different part of the brain. I do not—as far as anyone knows—reduce its chemical or electrical strength.

How could we distinguish knowing that we know something and believing that we know something? These are all words. They can make sense in particular circumstances—just as I hope the previous sentence made sense—but they are simply statements about states of affairs, not descriptions of different brain states and processes or different forms of understanding. The only way to tell the difference between knowledge and opinion, between fact and belief, is through knowledge. And the fact that thinking critically discloses that the statement I have just made is an endless regression—that further knowledge will always be required to distinguish knowledge and belief—makes my point.

The difference between facts and opinions is relative.[1] Nothing is certain—though some opinions may be better bets than others. But how do we know the better bets? Again, this is not a matter of skill, but of experience, and the ability to make judgments—another key word.

Judgment

Ennis employs the word *judging* eleven times in the list I cited on page 97, although many other lists and descriptions do not include the term at all. I do not think this discrepancy is because Ennis takes a wholly unique approach. In fact, in another list he constructed a few years later (cited by Beyer, 1985) the word *judging* is not used at all. But judgment is a useful all-purpose term that can be used as an alternative to all the scores of others that are employed in analyses of critical thinking.

When Dressel and Mayhew (1954) talk of "distinguishing verifiable and unverifiable data," for example, they could just as well have said "judging whether data are verifiable or unverifiable." "Detecting inconsistencies" (Fraser & West, 1961) could be reworded as "judging whether inconsistency exists"; "interpreting information" (Watson & Glaser, 1980), as "judging the implications of information"; and "recognizing biased statements" (Morse & McCune, cited by Beyer, 1985), as "judging that statements are biased."

Even Beyer's own "definition" of critical thinking—"determining the authenticity, accuracy, and worth of information or knowledge claims" (1985, p. 276)—could be revised to "judging the authenticity, accuracy, and worth of information or knowledge claims." Are five different things being done in the five quotations I have just paraphrased, or are distinguishing, detecting, interpreting, recognizing, and determining really only what English stylists would call *elegant variation* for the same act of judging? Acts of judgment could be seen as the common basis of all the so-called skills of critical thinking.

Common usage associates the term *critical thinking* with a judgmental attitude, and if any importance can be attached to definitions, the dictionary provides support. A critic is defined as "a judge," and being critical as "exercising judgment"—especially, it is interesting to note, "fault-finding" and "censorious." It is perhaps no wonder that "critical thinkers" are not universally popular.

But judgment is not a generalizable skill. A good judge of horses is not necessarily a good judge of ice skating or of art. Ability to judge on a particular occasion depends on the demands of the occasion—and there is no way anyone could acquire wide-ranging "judging" or "judgmental" skills. Judgment is not a unique psychological process; it is an aspect of the fundamental way in which we perceive the world. It is an attitude.

We are continually comparing our experiences of the world with alternative images and explanations that we ourselves generate. Whether or not such behavior is regarded as "critical thinking" depends not so much on what we are doing as on the circumstances in which we do it. Life continually demands judgment—and all of the other operational terms of critical thought. The extent to which we are actually critical on any particular occasion depends to some extent on what we will settle for.

People are called critical thinkers if they judge the assertions and behaviors of others—and the beliefs and behavior of themselves—in particularly pertinent and crucial ways. But making judgments is not an unusual or esoteric activity; everyone engages in judgmental behavior all the time. We judge when it is safe to cross the road, whether we want to go out to lunch, whether to commend (or criticize) a particular movie, and whether it is likely to rain tomorrow. We may not be perpetually on guard for exaggerated statements by our colleagues or for misleading claims in television commercials, but that is not because we are unable to make such judgments. Much of the time such thinking would not be appropriate, or its subject is so mundane that it never occurs to us that we might be doing anything particularly clever. Outrageous claims and observations immediately seize our attention—an indication that we are always in a relaxed state of critical watch—but we tolerate sloppy or biased thinking in the same way that we tolerate a moderate degree of background noise or variation in ambient temperature, not because we are insensitive, but because the discrepancy does not warrant special action or attention.

There are some matters we are all sensitive to, in our own way. Many people instantly detect racist or sexist bias in anything they see or hear. Others are totally insensitive to such concerns but would immediately be aware if their own chauvinistic feelings were challenged or their political beliefs taunted. We are all, in our own way, sensitive to assumptions of people we listen to or read, aware of their intentions and expectations, and ready to consider alternatives. These are not skills we need to be taught, though we might certainly need to have our sensitivities extended. We often fail to detect bias, fallacies, or manipulation in what we hear or read for the simple reason that they correspond with bias, fallacies, or points of view that we already have ourselves. We rarely demand that other people display their evidence if we agree with what they are saying.

Creative Thinking and Critical Thinking

The topic of judgment provides a convenient link for comparing those aspects of thinking commonly called *critical* and those called *creative*. In the previous chapter I characterized creative thinking in terms of the generation and selection of alternatives. Creative thinkers can both generate a wide range of relevant alternatives and select among them for the most appropriate one. But the same applies to critical thinkers. We all have specifications that generate in us certain alternatives to what we hear and read—but selectively blind us to other aspects.

I also argued that, apart from certain limited metaphorical extensions, generative and selective aspects of thought are in fact only regarded as creative if they are conducted by people categorized as artists, in certain "artistic" circumstances or surroundings, or with certain kinds of intention or motivation. But the same remarks apply to critical thought, which is identified in that way only if manifested by people categorized as "critical," in certain circumstances or surroundings, and with certain kinds of intention and motivation. Critical thinking is done by critics rather than by artists (except when the artists are acting as critics), although critics should be creative (just as artists must be critical). The generation of alternatives is a creative activity, and the selection among them must be critical. You may be called *creative* if you think of alternatives for your own behavior but *critical* if you do the same for others. The behaviors are the same; only the words are different.

The scores of qualifying terms that I have cited in relation to thinking in this chapter all involve the generation of alternatives and selection among them. The appropriate choice of word depends (apart from stylistic considerations) not on what a person is actually doing, but on the circumstances in which it is done and the reasons for doing it. There is no dictionary definition or behavior description that will differentiate between creative and critical thought because the choice of term depends on circumstances, not on semantics.

Critical and creative thinking may be viewed academically as unique mental activities, in which individuals can be deficient, but the elements of thinking critically and creatively are in everyone's behavioral and cognitive repertoire. People may often not appear to be thinking critically or creatively because they are often not in situations that permit or call for criticism or creativity, or because they are not disposed to behave critically or creatively in such situations. This does not mean that some individuals are totally incapable of thinking critically or creatively, or that they lack training. It is just that they are not thinking in those ways, for one reason or another.

HOW TO THINK CRITICALLY

If critical thinking is not a unique set of skills, if it is essentially something that everyone is capable of, that everyone does in some measure all the time, why does critical thinking—or its apparent absence—attract such attention? I have a few more remarks to make about specific knowledge, which is at the heart of the ability to be a critical thinker. But there are two other factors to take into account in explaining why some people might not appear to be as critical in their thought as they might be. One of them I have briefly alluded to already, the matter of disposition. The other is more contentious—the extent to which anyone is *allowed* to be a critical thinker. In other words—how serious all this talk about critical thinking is in the first place.

Knowledge

In an important book entitled *Critical Thinking and Education*, John McPeck (1981) makes a revealing comparison between thought and language. Language, he says, is not an abstract set of rules that can be applied in any situation. Instead, language is always about something. It makes no sense to talk about language—or an individual's language ability—without reference to what the language is about. Language always has a purpose as well as a content. If you do not understand what you are trying to talk about, then you will look as if you do not know how to talk.

The same applies to thinking, according to McPeck. Thought is not an abstract set of rules that can be applied in any situation. Instead, thinking is always about something, and it always has a purpose. If you do not understand what you are trying to think about, then you will look as if you do not know how to think.

To reiterate the point I have made so often in this chapter, all thinking depends on knowledge. Provided we know enough, we are always capable of *critical thinking* (I use the term here because McPeck uses it). But if we can make no sense of what we are trying to think about, then critical thinking is impossible.

Critical thinking does not demand a complex array of learned skills, but competence in whatever you are thinking about. If you understand cooking, you can be critical of the way a meal is prepared. If you are an experienced football fan, you can criticize a football game. If you are a particular kind of engineer, you can criticize the way a bridge or a ship has been built. If you are unable to do any of these things, it will not be because you lack essential critical thinking skills, but because you lack the essential experience. You do not know enough.

McPeck also argues that critical thinking is not a unique kind of thinking, but rather the effect that thinking has—critical—on a particular kind of occasion. He compares thinking about something critically with singing a song sensitively. We can think critically about innumerable things, he says—which means that we can think critically in innumerable ways.

McPeck's conclusion is that critical thinking is a disposition rather than a skill, a tendency to behave in particular ways on particular occasions. I have noted that Beyer comes to a similar conclusion with his own definition (or description?) of critical thinking as a matter of "determining the authenticity, accuracy, and worth of information or knowledge claims." Because of his skills orientation, Beyer calls this a *process*, suggesting a particular sequence of *operations* (another word he uses) that produces or causes critical thinking. But with the flexibility of language one could also say that critical thinking is a desire for, or propensity toward, or even habit of, determining the authenticity, accuracy, and worth of information or knowledge claims. Critical thinking is an attitude, a frame of mind.

Disposition

McPeck does not say that there are people who are not disposed to think critically at all, but that all of us are more or less disposed to think critically on particular occasions. McPeck sees this disposition as one of "reflective skepticism"—the *judicious* suspension of assent, a readiness to consider alternative explanations, not taking anything for granted when it might be *reasonable* to doubt.

The qualifications are important. The readiness to doubt has to be "reasonable" and "judicious." You do not become a critical thinker by disputing everything in sight—that would disable you as a thinker. You have to be reasonable—which means that we have still not escaped the primacy of knowledge. You have to *know* when it is reasonable to doubt. Values, feelings, even compromises, must be taken into account. Something has to control every flow of critical thought—and that control must lie in the intentions, the worldview, of the individual. Thinking critically is not a mechanical process to be switched on at appropriate times, but an inseparable part of thought on every occasion. The extent to which it is applied depends less on ability than on *willingness* to doubt—and to confront the consequences of that doubt. The opposite of a critical thinker is a passive, compliant individual.[2]

Doubt, like willingness and reasonableness, is not a skill, but a disposition. (Advocates of teaching critical thinking skills have not yet begun testing and training children in doubting and trusting skills.) Readiness to doubt depends not just on knowledge, or even on the particular situation in which doubt might reasonably be exercised. It depends on a cluster of personal factors such as perseverance, tolerance of ambiguity and uncertainty, readiness to pause and reflect, the postponement of gratification, openness to controversy, relationships with other people, and image of oneself. One might question the extent to which education, at every level, contributes positively to such factors, as opposed to encouraging passivity and compliance.

Critical thinkers must be ready to doubt, to challenge what is held to be true. From an extensive survey of the development of human thought, Boorstin (1985) concluded that the greatest obstacle to discovery is "the illusion of knowledge," what people already believe. I was tempted to begin this chapter with a quotation from the eighteenth-century critical thinker Vico, who said that the first thing to be done in thinking about anything is to ask whether it really exists; otherwise, the concern is only with a name (Covino, 1988, pp. 65-66).

From a slightly different perspective, readiness to think critically, the circumstances in which we are prepared to think critically, and the very manner in which we will think critically, all depend on the stories that we believe. Critical thinking reflects the way we perceive the world; its concern is not with the solution of "problems" but with the recognition of prejudices and biases—including our own. The beginning must be the old Greek adage "Know yourself."[3]

The very complexity of these matters illustrates that thinking in critical ways involves far more than learning a set of skills. Such a reductionist attitude could only interfere with the development and expression of critical thought, by focusing on extraneous "training" aspects and ignoring essential situational, individual, social—and political—factors.

Authority

Even given the ability and the readiness to exercise critical thought on a particular occasion, it may still be difficult to do so. There is one other essential prerequisite for thinking critically, and that is authority. The right to engage in critical thought is not distributed equally, especially in hierarchical, authoritarian, and bureaucratic societies. You could lose your job or your promotion, or your colleagues might find you less agreeable to work with.

One reason the term *critical thinker* is not used very much outside of the rituals of education may be because it is not particularly complimentary. A critical disposition is not generally regarded as an endearing character trait. Critical thinkers are *critical*; they are argumentative and unsettling; they rock the boat. They can have difficulty treading the line between constructive inquiry and nitpicking trouble-making. They may not always be comfortable to know.

Some of history's most critical thinkers—Socrates, Jesus, Galileo, and hosts of unnamed others—met cruel fates at the hands of their contemporaries. Extreme persecution for even moderately challenging views is far from unknown in contemporary life. Critical thinking challenges the status quo. One wonders how serious are some of the people who want more critical thinking, especially in education.

The right to engage in critical thought is not distributed equally in hierarchical institutions—and educational systems are among the most hierarchical institutions there are. The people at the *top* of the educational hierarchy (and there is no need to explain the metaphor) actually call themselves the *decision makers*, while those *lower down* (again, note the metaphor) are expected to "implement policy."

One way students could learn about critical thinking would be to observe their teachers exercising it, by having the opportunity to be "members of the club." The critical thought that students must see has to *matter*; that is why education itself could be such an appropriate focus for the demonstration and development of thinking critically. It is enlightening to consider what students currently learn about critical thinking from the way they see their teachers behave—and from the nature of the tests and instructional programs that come into classrooms in the name of critical thought (selected by teachers and administrators who should presumably be thinking critically themselves).

Tests and instructional materials related to critical thinking frequently consist of trivial puzzles, selected to be easy for some students and difficult for others (so that an appropriate "range" is achieved). The students who are regarded as good critical thinkers are those who do well on the tests, which are concerned with hypothetical and even improbable situations. One reason that critical thinking is broken down into numerous components is to make it fit into the constraining framework of current testing and instructional technology. Did the designers of such packages themselves become thinkers by learning to select the odd man out, the geometrical design that does not belong, or the best way to ferry missionaries and cannibals across a river? Could such considerations ever authorize anyone to think critically? The expectation that students and teachers should follow rigid guidelines of exercises, tests and discrimination might be seen as the antithesis of fostering critical thought.[4]

Critical Thinking and Language

Critical thinking is inseparable from language, not only because critical thought is frequently applied *to* language—analyzing statements, assertions, and "information"—but also because it is expressed through language. An unheard (or unread) critical thinker is practically a contradiction in terms.

Critical thinkers must not only reason, they must give reasons; they must not only evaluate arguments, they must argue. They must recognize, and engage in, techniques of persuasion. Effective critical thought is largely a rhetorical exercise. Uncritical passivity in thought and expression go hand in hand.

There is no doubt that the world could do with much more critical thinking. If critical thinking leads to better judgments, fewer problems, and happier consequences, then it is not just children and youth that are in need. It is unlikely that they will become better thinkers by uncritically emulating adults. The development of critical thinking requires a major shift across the generations, and the basis of that shift—if it is not to be catastrophic—must be through language.

Children and youth can hardly be blamed for the racism, terrorism, injustice, discrimination, war, pollution, poverty, brutality, exploitation, and famine that daily remind us that all is far from well in the way people think about the world. Children learn to think critically when they have opportunities and reason to think in critical ways; when they see (or hear) others engaged in critical thinking; and when they are admitted into arguments, challenges, and debates based on respect rather than power or exploitation.

8

THINKING AND LANGUAGE

Much of this book has been devoted to the complicated and often misleading way language categorizes thinking in its various guises. The present chapter has a more general concern with how language *expresses* thought and how thought is influenced by language.

The focus is on *uses*, not on *functions*. It is more common for theorists to talk of the functions of language and of thought than of their uses, but the choice of word is unfortunate. Uses are always much broader than functions, and usually far less contentious. The word *function* carries overtones of purpose and propriety, of concern with why something was developed rather than with how it has actually been found useful. The function of automobiles is to transport people and objects, but they are used for a variety of other purposes—as homes, offices, bedrooms, henhouses, jetties, breakwaters, even offensive weapons. The function of knives is to cut, though they can be used as paperweights, bookmarks, and ornaments. The function of objects tells us nothing about people (except the purposes of the objects' designers); the uses to which objects are put can tell a great deal about the users.

Conjectures about *how* thought developed, and *why* it developed, are based on speculation and ignorance. No one knows the original purposes of thought. Perhaps it has no purpose at all; it just came about accidentally. Perhaps, on the other hand, it is part of some great unknowable design. Asking the function of thought is like asking "Why are we here?"—there is no evidence, no way of settling controversies, and a multiplicity of opinions. On the other hand, *what* people do with thought is usually evident. There is far less mystery, and no mystique. The behavior of people can reveal what they think about and where their thinking leads them.[1]

The same applies to language. Excursions into *why* we have language, into what language is supposed to do, have been a source of endless and pointless professional and amateur speculation, fascinating and even amusing (including "bow wow" and "ding dong" theories), none of it verifiable or useful. Assertions about the functions of language can be egregiously misleading (as I argue for the contention that the function of language is to communicate) and dangerously authoritarian (when it is asserted that language should be employed in particular ways). Discussions of language function arouse passionately ideological emotions—or they bore. On the other hand, the uses to which language can be put are rich and multifarious, imaginative, idiosyncratic, and *evident*—a continually revealing source of ideas and possibilities.

The word *uses* in the context of thought has its problems, however, since it might be taken to imply that thinking can be separated from people (or people separated from thought). People do not literally use thought, nor do they use their brains to think. They think. *Thought* thinks, thought *is*, it uses itself. A rather clumsy way to escape this semantic spaghetti is to talk about what thought *does*, rather than how it is used.

WHAT THOUGHT DOES

Thought is always a part of language, though there are substantial aspects of thought that do not involve language. Language cannot be separated from thought, although I shall try initially to treat them separately by talking about what thought in general accomplishes and what language in particular achieves.

The central theme of this entire book can be summed up in a single phrase: *Thought creates realities*. Any exhaustive attempt to describe the realities that thought can create would require descriptions of all the real and imagined worlds in which we live, which the imagination can generate. And the question "What are the ways in which these worlds can be created?" would demand nothing less than a complete description of human emotions and perceptual systems. The world as we know it could not exist without the presence of a perceiver (a proposition that some physicists would extend to the beginning of the universe). If there is a world that exists independently of minds, in ways that minds could not possibly contemplate, there is no way we can think about it.

Thought is complex and multifaceted. It cannot be separated into threads of memory, comprehension, learning, and reasoning, nor can it be partitioned into meaningful episodes. A slice of thought, however it is cut, tells us no more about thought as a whole than the glimpse of a few squares of a chessboard could give an inexperienced observer any idea of how the game of chess is played. Thought is emergent, more than the sum of its parts, with capabilities unpredictable from any hypothetical elements or structures. Thought is not better understood by the detailed analysis of small samples. The range and richness of everything that thought produces must be apprehended. I have already referred to the magnitude of that task in terms of the complexity of the "real world" that thought creates. But we can also consider the intricacy of the worlds that thought creates through language.

WHAT LANGUAGE DOES

I must first try to dispel the misconception that the most important use—or primary function—of language is to communicate. Language generally does other things, and it does them better. In fact, natural languages (the languages that we all learned so effortlessly in childhood) are not very good for purposes of communication. They are not very effective for the unambiguous communication of information, of facts, knowledge, or data (even if the brain were particularly interested in that kind of thing). Artificial languages have to be devised for those purposes. All natural languages are superbly good at what thought strives to achieve all the time: the creation of realities, full not of information but of the possibilities of experience.

The reason language is so ineffective for conveying information is its ambiguity and lack of direct correspondence with the world. Language provokes the imagination rather than delineating what we might actually perceive. I have given many examples of the imprecision and fecundity of language in this book, especially with respect to the word *thinking*. But it is not only in respect of such abstract concepts that language fails; it has considerable limitations with the concrete as well. If we want to tell someone how to get somewhere, we are usually more successful drawing a map. For building a house, or fixing plumbing or wiring, sketches and plans are more efficient. A picture is better (than a thousand words?) in describing the details of a landscape. Mere words cannot convey how a person looks, or a flower smells, or a meal tastes. Technical books contain diagrams, illustrations, charts, and tables because words are so inadequate. Computers, which are pathetically unimaginative devices, cannot be addressed in everyday language at all, unless it is artificially constrained or "translated" (by a human) into an unambiguous code. We can never adequately express feelings in words;

we can say we are happy, but not what happiness feels like. Language always needs to be interpreted; it is never explicit.[2]

Spoken language is such a poor instrument for the transmission of information that it must be supplemented by gestures, postures, glances, grimaces, shrugs, grunts, and other forms of emphasis. And still people ask us to clarify what we mean. The more subtle the intent, the more it must be expressed nonverbally. Babies communicate perfectly well without language, and adults who cannot get themselves understood revert to more direct (and infantile) ways of expression. Language cannot be specific. The philosopher Karl Popper (1976) observes that precision in language can only be achieved at the cost of clarity.

Written language is even more opaque than speech, despite its undeserved reputation for lucidity. Written language lies wantonly on the page, oozing equivocation. The codification of laws leads to litigation rather than consensus; there were no lawyers before there was writing. Sacred texts become subject to exegesis the moment they are written down. When we try to force language to settle some of the confusion it creates, it bursts its seams. If a twenty-page memorandum does not make objectives clear, the common practice of expanding the document to forty pages doubles the uncertainty. Reducing a statement to a few pages—or preferably a few sentences—reduces disputation because there is less to argue about.

When we do want to put unambiguous information into language, we have to strip most of the grammar and semantic richness out of it. The telephone directory has a minimal grammar (sentence ⇒ name + address + number) with no possibility of stylistic variation, but little likelihood of idiosyncratic interpretation. I have yet to hear anyone debating the meaning of telephone numbers. On the other hand, despite miserable constraints on grammar, vocabulary, and style, bureaucratic documents seem always susceptible to misinterpretation, deliberate or accidental. "Simplifying" texts usually only makes them more difficult to read. Numbering paragraphs and sentences does not render them any less bewildering, especially when they are compressed into nested systems—"paragraph B.4.3(a)" or "page 2/7/3," to take examples from a government document and a computer manual that happen to be on my desk. Yet these mazes are seriously promoted as means of facilitating clarity and comprehension by people who think that giving text the inflexibility of a telephone directory will give it the same clarity.

Despite the bureaucratic myth, putting something in writing rarely helps to get it accomplished. It is often a good way of getting an idea filed away, passed on, or otherwise ignored. Documents can be more meaningful than their contents. The words on a birthday card do not usually convey a meaningful message—but sending the card does. Telephone calls may not do much for mutual understanding, but the *fact* that a call is made can express the message or make manifest the interest.

It appears almost perverse that natural language just does not seem suited to representing and communicating the "data" with which an electronic and bureaucratic world is becoming increasingly concerned. More and more people work with information about the world rather than with the world directly. They work with numbers and categories that treat "knowledge" as impersonal objects rather than as sources of subjective understanding. Such people are not usually working with language from which worlds can be constructed. Information, as every clerical worker knows, is not the same as experience, nor, paradoxically enough, is it usually as informative as experience. It does not lead to wisdom.

So what does language do? Why should it be so universally inexact when any competent communications engineer could easily shape it into an effective information-processing system? The answer is that language does best what thought must do—it creates realities.

LANGUAGE AND STORIES

Language enables us to put together and express the stories that make our lives meaningful, in whatever culture we live. If we had no stories, we would not have the kind of thought we have. Language, like art, enables alternative realities to be constructed, offering possibilities of experience that are not always available in the real world.

Language enables us to create the stories we need to make sense of experience and to share experience. With language we can set the stage, paint backdrops, depict scenes, introduce characters, reflect on intentions and emotions, and understand conflicts and outcomes. This is not "information," except in the most trivial and incidental sense—this is the making of events. "Communication" does not take place when these events are experienced by other people, except, again, in the most trivial and metaphorical sense. The information communicated to me by the debris of a traffic accident is only a small and incidental part of my experience when I encounter the scene, in fact or in the pages of a novel.

If thought did not have language, it could not create many of the worlds that we experience and share. We cannot hold thoughts in our head for more than a few moments, and we cannot display them for the benefit of others without language (or art) to give them shape. Language stands still while the world moves on, allowing us to experience something many times, in instant replays of reality.

Language, in ways complementary to those of the visual arts, permits the creation of landscapes more complex than those of nature because they can encompass ideas. But in essence the constructions of language, or of art, are no different from the constructions we find in or put into "reality." They give rise to the same kinds of perceptions, desires, understandings, and emotions. I described, in Chapter 4, how all external events impinge on the brain as undifferentiated bursts of neural impulses, independently of whether the scene we are focusing on is in a book, on a canvas, or in the material world. Everything has to be interpreted, put into life, and experienced in the great common theater of the imagination.

We move in an identical manner through the realities of language, visual art, and the physical world. Trees in language and in art are the same as trees in the real world; they are related in the same ways to everything else that we understand. The objection that an apple in a story cannot be eaten the way "real apples" are eaten is mistaken; apples in stories can be eaten by characters in stories and are just as nourishing for them. Everything is made possible by the particular reality in which it is located.

It is true that different people will respond to a story in different ways, just as they will respond to pictures in different ways—but they also respond to the real world in different ways. Language is always interpreted, but so is the real world, and life itself. Any meaningfulness that we find in our own experience is what we put there (which is the reason that raw existential experience is so nihilistic and depressing—the moment we look for meaning, rather than putting it there, we confront a formless, purposeless void).

Language is more powerful than reality. Within very narrow limits, the physical world cannot be manipulated, certainly not by individuals. We may interpret it differently, but to a large extent we must take it as we find it. Language, however, can be tailored to our own desires and interests. We can construct alternative worlds. We can share them. We do not have to be "literal," in fact language works best through metaphor, through "figures of speech." In the real world, the only metaphors we can find are those we put there—and we permeate our realities with the metaphors that language makes possible.[3]

Language permits the imagination and the emotions to flourish. While language cannot directly depict feelings, or transfer them from one person to another, it makes empathy possible, the reconstruction of an experience that will generate similar feelings. We talk of this—in a loose way—as "communicating feelings," though what we are really doing is making it possible for similar feelings to be aroused in other people. We do not experience the feelings of the author when we read, even when we read an autobiography. We experience our own feelings, the way we make sense of what we read, by projecting our own understanding onto it.

I cannot *tell* you what it is like to be in a frightening or exciting situation. But I can—if I am a skillful enough writer—create situations in which you can have those experiences. If you want to convey a feeling of what it is like to be a student or a teacher at a particular school, description will not suffice; but a novel or short story might.

Most of the beliefs we have about the world and our place in it come in the form of stories. Most of the beliefs we have about other people, and the way we regard and treat them, are in the form of stories. Stories are the mortar that holds thought together, the grist of all our explanations, rationales, and values.[4]

Thought is inseparable from a literally fabulous conglomeration of personalized stories—religious, political, social, economic, philosophical, and psychological. Language underlies our beliefs and attitudes concerning nature, animal rights, war, education, welfare, nuclear energy, meat-eating, freedom of speech—any issue on which we have an opinion or can take a position. These opinions are often weakly based on data or incontrovertible facts. Instead we look for, and focus on, evidence that supports our opinions, that is congruent with our stories.

Armies, terrorists, and bigots are motivated by the stories they believe—and so are peacemakers, philanthropists, and martyrs. We do not have to look deeply into ourselves to mobilize our prejudices; they come forward silently and unbeckoned, always on cue, shaping our beliefs and actions, as our imagination constantly constructs and interprets our world.

In considering the influence of language on how we think, we should not overlook language in the form of songs. Out of curiosity, I recently listed the titles of all the songs whose words I could remember. These are mostly popular radio and movie tunes of my adolescence that still come into my head when I least expect them and often when I least need them. I wrote out more than 300 titles without difficulty, and they are still coming. I am not proud of all these lyrics that I learned without even trying. Most of them are trite, and some are offensive. There are strong veins of mawkish sentimentality and blind chauvinism running through them, encumbering weeds that I would rather not have cluttering my mind. But at the time I learned those songs I *believed* them, and in return they have stayed with me. They became part of my stories.

Language need not be as complex as it is for communication, for the transmission of information. Its complexity, as I have tried to show, defeats precision. "Correct" language is a cultural construction, a matter of convention, not a product of logic or rationality. Natural languages have developed as cultural systems of great intricacy and subtlety, but so have our systems of dress, ornamentation, furnishings, and house and office design, not because of efficiency or economy, but because of the images we can create with them, the stories they make possible, the experiences they provide for ourselves and others.

Telling stories is not the only thing language does that is not communication. Language also makes many things happen. When someone says "I name this ship *Stella Maris*," or "I now pronounce you husband and wife," the statements are not communicating the fact that the ship is named or that the marriage has taken place. The statements actually cause the ship to be named, or the couple to be married. Such statements are technically known as *performatives*; they are *acts* rather than statements. They constitute events in the world. Such statements cannot be true or false. They also cannot make sense, in the way stories make sense. They are like the laying on of hands in a ritual, or shaking hands on a deal, or putting our signature on a document—they change the state of the real world.[5]

THOUGHT AND LANGUAGE

A widespread point of view is that language is a necessary precursor of thought, both in individuals and in the evolution of humanity. Babies are often assumed to be incapable of thinking before they can talk. But it is thought that enables babies to talk. They could not understand their first words if they could not think about what the purpose and the meaning of those words might be. Adults who cannot talk can still think.[6]

It has also been widely argued that written language has changed the way the human mind works—that literacy enables us to think in new and more powerful ways.[7] But it is the possibility—or at least the potential—of thinking in certain extended ways that opens the door to language in written form. Literacy does not require or develop a different kind of human thought any more than automobiles require or develop different kinds of legs—although automobiles, with their foot pedals, have certainly extended the range of things that legs can accomplish.

One theory of the way that language determines thought, including our basic manner of perceiving the world and categorizing experience, is the *linguistic relativity hypothesis*. This theory—also known as the *Whorfian hypothesis*, after its primary exponent, Benjamin Lee Whorf (1956)—asserts that we do not share the world we inhabit with everyone, but only with those who have the same language habits as ourselves. I have already alluded to this hypothesis with reference to all the "thinking" words that have cropped up in this book.

The relativity hypothesis does not assert that English speakers could not discuss snow or horses with the precision of Eskimos or Arabs, who have many more words in those categories, but that the English speakers would have to use more complex circumlocutions; discussion would not be so easy for them. The hypothesis also does not assert that we will be unable to see differences or categories that are not represented in our own language; only that we will be less likely to pay attention to them. I am well acquainted at the moment with a small bird that appears outside my window most mornings. I can describe that bird—small, brown, sharp-beaked, dark-headed, white-breasted—with words in my current vocabulary, but I do not have a specific name for it. My difficulty in trying to talk about the bird should be apparent.

The way in which we organize our perceptions of the world—the way we create that world—obviously reflects our past experience, and even more the experience of others in the culture to which we belong. The languages of communities and cultures are distillations of their experience and also the means by which this experience is passed from one generation to another. Language develops to match the thinking of the people who use it, not the information they have acquired, and in turn it shapes their thinking. The history of a language and the history of the culture that uses that language are inseparable.

The meaning of our life is in our language, and the meaning of language is in our stories, in the way we have constructed the world for ourselves. There have been many attempts to construct theories of meaning—usually trying to find meaning in language itself, or in the world around us, as if those were the only two choices.

But linguists have demonstrated that meaning cannot lie in language itself; it is too complex, ambiguous, and incomplete. Chomsky (1972) distinguished the "surface structure" of language (roughly speaking, the parts that we can hear and see, whether or not we understand the language) from the "deep structure" (where meaning resides, in the minds of language users). As psychologist George Miller (1962) has pointed out, individual words frequently have alternative meanings, alone and in groups (as with puns), while different words can have the same meanings (as with synonyms and paraphrases). Context—including the listener's or reader's expectations—determines the meaning and often makes alternative interpretations (including what the speaker or writer might have intended) unsuspected. Speakers and listeners generate the meanings that language appears to convey, rather than the actual words that pass between them.

But what is the basis of the meaning that we all put into the language that we understand? It cannot be the world around us, not directly, despite "theories of reference" that relate the meaning of language to the world. As I have frequently had to demonstrate in this book, the words we use may have nothing to do with actual "facts" or with reality; they do not necessarily refer to something that "exists" outside of language. That does not mean that words are forced to float meaninglessly in language, but that any reality that words have must reside in thought, in the worlds we construct in the head. We relate words to the categories that the mind constructs, not to categories that can be found in the world. Occasionally, words never get outside language. They are not even related to distinctive mental categories; they only find their place among other words. These are the words, like "thinking," that are forever the subject of definitional debates.

This is not to say that "abstract" words are the most difficult to understand or use in everyday life. Abstract words (or abstract "concepts") are supposed to be more difficult to understand than concrete ones, especially for children, but that depends entirely on context. We have no problem with abstraction when someone says to us "That's not the truth" or "The verdict was just"—although we might have difficulty saying what truth or justice *is*. On the other hand, nothing could be more concrete than "Give me your vote"—yet it can lead to deep and difficult thought.

The realities that language constructs (including the Whorfian reality) are not in the world, they are in our head. Thought mediates between language and the objective world. Words become woolly when we take them to be an objective map of what is in the world. Words are maps of the way we think. Meanings, and thought, are abstractions.

Thought must be far more than language. If thought were only language, how could we understand the language that is thought? Synonyms and paraphrases do not tell us what words and phrases mean, they merely provide alternative words. The meaning has to be found beyond language.

Unfortunately, a number of specialists talk metaphorically about languages inside the head. Linguistic philosopher Jerry Fodor (1975) discusses the "language of thought"—a propositional structure nothing like the language we talk (or he writes) that he nevertheless sees as the way thought is organized and (external) language understood. Neuro-scientist Karl Pribram (1971) talks about "languages of the brain"—the way different segments and sections "communicate" with each other. His language (and possibly Fodor's also) is neurological. But these are highly metaphorical uses of the words *language* and *communication*. Different parts of the brain interact, but not by "talking" with each other; they are interconnected. The pedals, brakes, and wheels of a car are interconnected; they do not talk to each other.

To argue that there is a language in the brain into which the lan-guages that we talk is translated is like arguing that life is a dream. We then have to find another term for the dreams we have in life to distin-guish them from the different order of dream that life itself is supposed to be. (In the same way, stories cannot be reduced to other stories. You are always left with a story to be understood; the understanding has not been explained.)

If there are languages in the brain that comprehend the language in the world around us, they are different orders of language. They are not languages that we can learn or use. They are not languages that are understood, either by ourselves or by the theorists who postulate them. The ultimate way in which thought understands or interprets language will probably always be a mystery, because we can only think about language in terms of language.[8]

THE RECLUSIVENESS OF THOUGHT

Thought is coy, concealing itself from ourselves and from others. We cannot spy on how other people think or how they perceive the world but must make deductions from their behavior and from what they say. If I am to learn whether someone knows the name of the prime minister of Bulgaria, or can program computers, or likes eating aspara-gus, I must ask or observe that person's behavior. Inspection of an individual's head, inside or out, reveals nothing of the contents of the mind, no matter how sophisticated the instruments used. CAT scans cannot reveal what patients are thinking.

But our own thought processes are equally inaccessible to us. We can no more review our own thinking procedures than we can look in on our metabolism. If I want to know whether I know the Bulgarian prime minister's name, or can program computers, or enjoy asparagus, I have to see whether I can produce the name, or write a computer program, or recall the fact that I can write computer programs or enjoy asparagus.

In other words, my thought has to produce something before I can know what I think; I cannot observe thinking itself, only its consequences.

Thought proceeds in absolute privacy. Human artifacts show us what thought does, the directions that thought takes. Works of art, music, and invention are products of thought—and so is the world as we perceive it. The ways in which we view other people, and life itself, are products of our thought and can be examined to expose the directions our own thought takes. Behavior also discloses the nature of thought, including the revealing behavior that is language. Our own thought can become apparent from what we say to others—and also from what we say to ourselves.

Talking to ourselves is often regarded as a bad habit, if not a sign of mental deterioration. But as far as my own informal researches have shown, we all talk to ourselves. Every time we listen we can hear our inner voice (or rather voices—language in the head is often a conversation, sometimes with an elaborate cast of characters). The language we hear in our head is sometimes confused with thought itself, but it is not. The conversations we have with ourselves are no different from the conversations we have with other people, except that one kind is more private. Both kinds are the result of thought, or the reflection of ongoing thought.[9]

We rarely think and then say what we have thought (and if we do, our speech probably sounds artificial and labored). Thought is the driver in immediate control of the journeys of language, not the dispatcher in a distant operations room. We think as we speak or write, to ourselves or to others. We might occasionally think about what we are going to talk about, but not about how we will say it. If we pause to consider how we will enter a discussion, we usually fail to get in. The flow of conversation—or of thought itself—usually precludes preplanning. Usually we do not know how a sentence will end when we begin it. We talk, and our thought progresses. Watch preachers and lecturers who are not reading from notes or reciting a well-rehearsed ritual. No one could be more interested in hearing what these speakers will say than they are themselves.

The voices in our head are not thought, but they reflect thought and facilitate it. We rehearse conversations we had—or might have had—in the past. We anticipate conversations we will have—or might have, or might even prefer not to have—in the future. Inner speech is experience, just like the more public kind.

But to create and explore experience, thought needs more than language, and more than real or imaginary casts of characters to employ language. Thought needs sets and props. It needs imaginary worlds. The images and scenes that we construct in the seclusion of our mind, our daydreams and fantasies, are just as much products of thought as the inner voices that we hear. They reflect thought, and facilitate it, but they are not thought itself. Thought lies beyond images; images do not explain language.

Just as the meaning of anything we hear or read must lie beyond language, so the meaning of anything we see, or imagine, must lie beyond a visual experience. We do not understand the nature or relevance of a cow in a field by consulting an illustration of a cow in a field that we keep in our minds. Images are constructs of thought, not thought itself.

Experimental psychologists sometimes ask their subjects to provide commentaries on what they are thinking as they write or reflect on problems. But the reports the experimenters receive and analyze are not samples of thought; they are descriptions of images that ongoing thought generates. The situation can be quite artificial and even misleading. Trying to think about what we are thinking as we do something can be—like the centipede's curiosity about which leg to move next—a disturbing disruption. Thought has to flow. Self-examination of what we might do next, or of why we might have done the last thing, stops thought in its tracks. The reports that are made are not samples of thought but additional products of thought, and by their very nature products of thought that has been disturbed, not thought that is proceeding normally.

THOUGHT AND THE BRAIN

Thought is not accessible to direct inspection or introspection—nor does it disclose its secrets to incursions by the probes of neuroscientists. Attempts to explore thought by examining its physiological substructure have proved remarkably unrevealing. Dramatic discoveries have been made about how the parts of the human brain are put together, and about the kinds of chemical and bioelectrical processes that take place within the millions of bundles of nerve fibers of which it is comprised, but they tell us nothing about the nature of thought that was not known before. The operations of thought remain as unpredictable from the wiring inside the skull as the operations of computers, refrigerators, toasters, vacuum cleaners, and a multitude of other appliances are unpredictable from the wiring system of a house.

Particular aspects of thought are related to particular areas and conditions of the brain, but only in the most general way. The left side of the brain (in most people) is particularly involved in some aspects of language and in other "analytical" activities, while the right side seems more concerned with subjective and artistic matters. But none of us uses only half of the brain, and every activity in which we engage involves both objective and subjective elements, focal and global concerns. Some people are more aggressive and analytical, or more sensitive and reflective, than others, but this has long been known; it is everyday knowledge. To attribute such variation to left- or right-brain "dominance" explains nothing and is metaphorical at best.

There is a widespread concern in education today with "learning styles," allegedly related to particular functions of the brain. Once again, it is ancient wisdom that some people prefer looking at pictures to listening to music, or would rather read a book than watch a movie, but that does not mean that they can only learn through specific modalities. Learning involves all our sensory systems, and all our feelings as well. No one can just learn visually, or aurally. It is as simplistic to regard reading as a purely visual activity as it would be to regard the understanding of speech as an auditory event. When we learn to talk, we relate the sounds of language to our interpretations of the sounds, sights, smells, tastes, and feel of events going on around us.[10]

Neuroscientific insights into brain processes and mechanisms in limited medical or scientific settings are frequently "translated" into broad educational statements. These extrapolations are usually made by educators with only a superficial understanding of neurophysiology, or by neuroscientists with no profound knowledge of language, teaching, or learning. Brain theories are used as explanations for educational failure—even as excuses for that failure—in the absence of any direct evidence that children are incompetent learners. Learning is a social activity,[11] and it has long been known (though frequently ignored) that there are social and other interpersonal reasons why some children might find school irrelevant and confusing. Pseudoscientific learning theories are a convenient way of blaming the victim.

It is not coincidental that the areas of brain research that are drawn upon to account for social and educational inadequacies are the ones that are currently most prominent in the popular media. The theories have to be based on simplistic reasoning. The fact that certain parts of an intricate and highly interconnected brain can be grossly associated with patterns of thought and learning that are themselves infinitely subtle and complex says nothing about the nature of thought itself.

Educators have learned nothing from being told by brain researchers that cognition and perception involve complex and interrelated networks of thought—they should have known that before by simple observation. Scientists reveal that neural events are richly interconnected, through excitation, inhibition, and "spreading activation," but it has always been evident that mental events are connected ("trains of thought" used to be the popular metaphor). What the actual connection is between mental and neural sequences of events remains totally obscure. No one knows how a particular fact is represented in the brain, or a decision, let alone a preference or a doubt. No one even knows how to look for neurological or chemical correlates to such mental conditions.

Even if particular patterns of neural activity were discovered to be directly associated with particular sequences of mental events, what would that tell us about how people think? A neurosurgeon's probe might stimulate a particular neural complex and remind us of a song, or even make us sing it backwards, but what would that tell us about our knowledge of the song, or what the song means to us? To expect the hardware of the brain to reveal rich subtlety of human thought is like predicting the way a family lives from the way the floorboards of their home are nailed to the joists.

How can neural events explain *language*, or a story? Stories explain themselves, and they explain the way people think and behave. Neuroscience only adds mystery.

It has been argued that neurologists and physiologists have been unable to talk about the relationship between mind and matter because they are not asking the right questions. But it is impossible to know what those questions should be. What exactly are we looking for when we try to find the process in the brain that results in the sensation of the color red, or the enjoyment of a symphony? What could the story of Robinson Crusoe possibly look like as a sequence of synaptic events? Chemistry is clearly involved in thought—but it does not explain how we distinguish bread from milk on the grocery list. Drugs may enhance or interfere with particular kinds of brain function, but until they can make us remember bread and forget milk—in other words, until they can become selective—they tell us nothing about thought.[12]

Thought does not reveal its secrets to surgical probes—but it does not have to. Neuroscientists ask (or should ask) kinds of questions different from those asked by psychologists, philosophers, and educators. Knowledge of structures of the brain is not required in order to understand the way people think, any more than knowledge of the structures of the leg can explain why some people go dancing and others prefer to swim.

Thought keeps its intimate secrets, and perhaps always will. But that does not mean that *people* cannot be better understood by attention to the individual ways in which they behave. It also does not mean that people's thinking cannot be changed, or at least influenced—an important consideration in a world of blindness, bigotry, stupidity, and *thoughtlessness*. There is one last issue to face, though certainly not to resolve, and that is how human thought might be made more effective, and more *humane*. There is the issue of education.

9

THINKING AND EDUCATION

The image of thinking that has developed in this book is one of a single, continual, all-embracing operation of the mind, powered by an imagination that never rests, not of a collection of disparate skills, some of which may be absent or deficient until they are taught. Learning, remembering, understanding, and other manifestations of thought—such as reasoning, problem-solving, and creative and critical thinking—are not separate mental faculties or skills, but reflections of a constantly driving imagination. Everyone can think. The deployment and effectiveness of thought on particular occasions depends on three critical considerations: the thinker's broad understanding of whatever matters are being thought about, disposition to think about those matters, and authority to do so.

Learning to think is less a matter of instruction than of experience and opportunity. Experience must provide familiarity with the topics and subjects that thought should address, and also the confidence that underlies the disposition and authority to think on particular matters.

Dispositions are idiosyncratic, matters of preference rather than ability. We are all disposed to think about some things but not about others—depending on our interest in them, and whether we *feel* they are within our competence. We are not born with specific dispositions to think about particular kinds of things; experience teaches where our predilections lie. The disposition to think about particular matters rises and falls on tides of positive and negative experience, on the perceived degree to which one can assert, or can gain, the right to think and to express one's thoughts. No one has to learn to think, any more than it is necessary to learn to learn, to remember, or to understand. Everyone is born equipped and ready to think and learn, as part of the continual exercise of the imagination that enables us to make sense of our world.

Like learning, the development of thinking depends on the company we keep; it depends on the way we perceive ourselves, which depends in turn on the way other people treat us. The development of how we think is affected by how we see people around us behave, and by the role we see for ourselves in their activities. When we are encouraged or inspired to engage in what other people are doing, when our own imagination is in control, then learning comes naturally and effortlessly, including everything that is essential about "learning to think." People become thinkers who associate with thinking people, including the thinking people who can be met through literature and art.

On such an analysis, educational institutions—from kindergarten to university—should be places where relevant and worthwhile thinking is embedded in every activity of the day, not as an exercise or subject matter, but as the way things are done. Teachers should demonstrate the power and possibilities of thought in everything they do, and by never engaging their students in meaningless, thoughtless activity. Students should be empowered to explore the power and possibilities of thought themselves, by seeing others explore, examine, question, and argue, and by being permitted to behave similarly.

Schools vary enormously in the thinking that can be seen to be done in them, and in the kinds of things that are thought about. There are no schools that are entirely good or bad, except in fanciful exaggeration. In all schools, probably, at least some teachers encourage and support useful thinking on the part of some students, some of the time. (By useful or worthwhile thinking, I mean opportunity to think creatively and critically about relevant and interesting topics, about things that make a difference, to the individual and to the world.) But also in all schools, some teachers some of the time doubtless discourage and undermine worthwhile student thought.

The question should not be how any school might become perfect. Despite the claims of educational evangelists, there is no evidence that "perfect" schools or "excellent" education are currently to be found or ever likely to exist. But perfection is not required. Obviously every teacher should try to do more that is worthwhile and constructive, and less that is pointless or destructive. But prior to that, and even more important, teachers and students should be able to *recognize* those aspects of education that facilitate effective thinking, and those that interfere with it. In other words, education must itself be the focus of critical thinking.

FACILITATING THINKING

Nothing in the analysis of thinking I have made helps a teacher—or an administrator—who believes that thinking can be taught through systematic instruction. Everything I have said, on the other hand, should support teachers and administrators who believe that students can be trusted to learn, and to think, provided the students are immersed in an environment that promotes and encourages thought. Facilitating thinking is more a matter of attitude than of lesson plans.

There can be no simple formula for teaching students to "think better," or to think more obviously in the creative and critical ways that are considered desirable. To learn to think more creatively, students must not simply be exposed to more "creative activities" themselves; they must associate with creative people in creative enterprises. I have no list of ideal or foolproof "creative enterprises" for students to be engaged in—the choice depends on the creative experience and propensities of the teacher (and the students) and on the creative interests of the people the teacher can bring into the classroom.

To learn to think more critically, it is similarly essential for students to be associated with challenging thinkers. A workbook on critical thinking is a contradiction in terms; one cannot think critically about trivial or purposeless matters.

Books are a traditional, obvious, and easy way to bring students into contact with creative and critical people. Writing is a traditional, obvious, and easy way to encourage students to become creative and critical themselves. Talk of all kinds (monologues, dialogs, discussions, debates, interviews, and arguments) and art of all kinds promote creative and critical thinking. But the reading, writing, talking, and art must always be accessible and unconstrained; it must not be used as a basis of evaluating performance or of discriminating among students. Students who think that reading, writing, and talking are risky activities in school are unlikely to engage in them in thought-provoking ways.

There are two characteristics of schools and classrooms in which worthwhile thinking and learning are facilitated. The first is *interest*. None of us can think effectively about anything we find boring and purposeless, nor can we learn anything that is worthwhile about such tedious matters. What we think, and learn, is that such matters are tedious.

Interest guarantees that we engage in thought and that we learn. We think and learn every time we read a newspaper or a novel, every time we engage in conversation or watch a movie, and every time we solve a problem or make a plan—provided we are interested. (Of course, if we read or watch trivial things, we think and learn trivial things.) The moment interest flags, we think of something else. Distractability shields us from pointless boredom; it ensures that we struggle to move to situations in which we can think and learn. Lack of comprehension also destroys the possibility of worthwhile thought—but lack of comprehension also destroys interest.

The phrase *think and learn* in the preceding paragraphs has been totally redundant and I shall not use it any more. Thinking is always accompanied by learning, because the brain learns all the time unless something is known already—and then boredom strikes. Learning is inseparable from thinking, because the brain strives to think all the time, and meaningful learning takes place when there is thought. Only rote learning is thought-less, but rote learning is also notoriously uninteresting and inefficient. Forgetting is guaranteed unless the rote learning is continually rehearsed, or committed to memory in the form of chants, rhymes, or jingles, like the multiplication tables and the number of days in the months.

Interest does not guarantee that we think efficiently, but it ensures that we put ourselves into situations where relevant thought is more likely to be demonstrated. When our interest is aroused, we strive to join the company of people involved in the activity that interests us; we read books and watch movies on the topic, and we see ourselves as "the kind of person" who engages in the interesting activity. We learn from the kind of people we see ourselves as being like—and we learn to think like those people.

Good classrooms are interesting classrooms—not because they command the active attention of teachers and the students, although they do, but because they make thinking possible and worthwhile, because imaginations can run free. There are always interesting topics and events to think about. It is a matter of the manner in which everything is done, rather than of what specifically is done.

The second characteristic of effective schools and classrooms is *respect*. There must be respect for those who are taught, and also for what is taught. All learning is social. (Even when we learn from books, we learn with the authors of the books—or with the characters in the books.) We learn not to think like the people whose groups we decide we are excluded from, that we never expect to join or want to join. Where there is no respect, thought is dominated by the lack of respect.[1]

When teachers respect the feelings and opinions of their students, then teachers and students become partners in whatever is thought about, to the advantage of both parties. A most productive partnership can arise when teachers and students together think about those educational circumstances that result in negative and unproductive thinking, rather than coming into conflict over them.

The key for teachers and for students is *empowerment*—the personal empowerment that comes with independence rather than submissiveness or resentment, the expressive empowerment that comes with a language that develops as it is valued, and the social empowerment that comes with authority. All these aspects of empowerment must be founded in respect.

INTERFERING WITH THINKING

Not everything that is done in schools—including universities—facilitates thinking. Independent thinking is hardly likely to occur when students are told precisely what they should learn, and what they should think about it. And students are also not likely to improve as independent thinkers when they see teachers themselves being told precisely what they should teach, and how they should teach it.

Reading and writing are two activities that promote thought—provided that what is read is worth thinking about and that writing is used for extending the imagination of the writer. Discussion promotes thought, but not when one side of every exchange is constantly evaluated as right or wrong. Thinking cannot be broken down into parts, specified in objectives, and taught in isolated exercises and drills. All of this interferes with thought.[2]

It is difficult to maintain interest when the content of the lesson is prescribed in detail by someone outside the classroom who cannot see whether the students (or the teachers) are bored or confused, cooperative or resentful, "morning people" or "afternoon people," hungry, anxious, bruised, or angry. It is difficult to maintain interest when students are grouped together on the basis of ability, so that they cannot help each other, and when the scope of their activities is confined by the constraints of timetables and the classroom walls.

The daily newspaper, or a novel, is a better stimulus to thought than textbooks and worksheets—even than those textbooks and worksheets that are labeled "thinking"—provided, of course, that the newspaper or novel is not used like a textbook or worksheet, or as the basis of a test.

Teachers cannot abdicate responsibility for what students think about or learn—either to the students themselves or to some authority or publisher outside the classroom. It is the teacher's role to ensure that students engage in worthwhile activities as much as possible. Thinking is facilitated by autonomous teachers who create situations and mutual enterprises that are interesting and relevant for everyone who is involved.

IMPROVING THINKING IN SCHOOLS

The first thing to be done to improve the quality of thinking in all educational institutions, from grade school to graduate school, is perhaps the most radical. Students—and teachers—must learn to doubt. Schools currently run on a basis of certainties that teachers are expected to transmit to students. Students are not expected to question what teachers tell them, or the contents of their textbooks—or "information" from computer databanks (a growing threat). Teachers are not expected to express uncertainty about what is taught. In universities especially, there are "authorities" in every subject who believe that they have corrected every error of the past—and that they will never be corrected in their turn.

Students learn from the way they are taught the illusion that "knowledge" exists, that it can be trusted (unless specifically labeled *myth* or *propaganda*), and that the transmitters of knowledge can be trusted. Students must have the opportunity to learn that knowledge can be challenged, that fact may be opinion, and that argument can be constructive. If they discover independently that transmitters of knowledge they have been taught to trust are not in fact trustworthy, there can be violent feelings of betrayal, anger, and rejection.

Certainty stunts thought, in ourselves and others. The fruits of understanding grow from seeds of doubt. All thinking is based on "suppose things were different." Critical thinking begins with readiness to challenge received wisdom. Creative thinking is the opposite of logic; it considers all alternatives and resists mechanistic modes of decision-making. Thought flourishes as questions are asked, not as answers are found.

A serious problem today is not so much demand for instant information or gratification as for instant decision and comment. There is little tolerance for uncertainty and doubt, in others and in ourselves. Thirty-second or three-paragraph "news items," five-second television clips, three-minute "interviews," and ten-minute "debates" encourage people to believe they should be able to take an immediate position on any topic. The consequence is a readiness to respond with slogans rather than with reflection. Students and teachers must learn not to be afraid of withholding judgment, of challenging the assertions of others, and of having their own ideas challenged in return. The opposite is tyranny and stultification.[3]

School should be fertile with questioning, not in the sense of teachers' constantly catechising students to assess how much they know, but of everyone's investigating contemporary reality to try to understand why it is the way it is. How will students learn to think clearly and boldly, especially about their own education? Only by seeing teachers engaging in thought in this way, beginning, as I have suggested, with a joint examination of the educational system itself.

It may be objected that it is not always useful or even practicable to doubt. A media report that an airliner has crashed probably means that an airliner has crashed, and students will not be able to go through life disbelieving everything they read and hear. It is true that we all have to take chances with our beliefs, but that does not mean that our beliefs should be undiscriminating. Experienced newspaper readers know that a report that an airliner has crashed does not necessarily mean that an accident occurred, or even that a plane actually crashed, especially if the report comes from a politically volatile region of the world, or if a political figure is supposed to have been on the flight.

One cannot go through life disbelieving everything—but it is only through experience that one learns the kinds of things that should be doubted, and the kinds of circumstances in which doubting is appropriate. No one (yet) has suggested that there is a way of teaching students "essential doubting skills." But they will learn from example.

Many systematic approaches to teaching thinking skills stress the importance of learning to distinguish fact from opinion. But as I have pointed out, there is no way to distinguish fact from opinion, except personal knowledge of whatever the fact or opinion is expressed about. There is no formula for determining whether items of news are fact or opinion. Matters labeled as facts are frequently opinions, and opinions can turn out to be facts. The educational problem is not that children cannot distinguish between fact and opinion, but that opinion is frequently presented as fact. Readers may occasionally draw inappropriate inferences from reports in newspapers and on television, but more often the problem is that they draw the precise inferences they were intended to draw. Duplicity is difficult to detect, especially when it is skillfully done, and when students—and teachers—are trained to trust experts and authorities.

Students are often criticized for inability to draw appropriate conclusions from scientific demonstrations and experiments. They do not lack essential thinking skills, but they (and their teachers) need a better understanding of science. The same applies to literature, and to politics. Often it is simply the language that is not understood, a lack that has to be remedied by experience, not by "teaching vocabulary."

Students must see teachers thinking—and teachers themselves must learn to think, by considering alternatives, engaging in argument, and challenging received ideas and preconceptions. A good way to begin to do this might be by a critical study of the language of education.

A substantial part of educational language is highly discriminatory—and it contaminates the way everyone in education thinks. Schools obviously best serve a narrow segment of society—the group that typically succeeds in school (and that must succeed, since all tests are normed on its representatives). Students from other groups—from different social or economic backgrounds, from minority populations, or who have physical conditions that differentiate them—are termed "deprived," "disadvantaged," "disabled," or "students with special needs," in contrast with the "mainstream" students. In other words, where there is a mismatch between schools and students, the language that is used automatically locates the deficiency in students rather than in schools. Special programs may be installed to help these students "catch up"—immediately identifying them as different, and as the cause of problems. If there is no place for such students in a regular classroom, the students (and their culture) are held responsible, not the way school systems are constructed.[4]

We could stop thinking of educational institutions as places where only those judged most fit survive, and start to think of them as communities of mutual respect; as sanctuaries from the pressures and inequalities of the world outside, not a proving ground for discrimination, segregation, and unfairness. The social organization of education could be reformed, from a hierarchical supervisory structure to one of cooperative support and advocacy. Responsible behavior should be expected as a natural consequence of freedom and respect, not as a prerequisite for them. The social (and thinking and learning) price of always making cost-effectiveness the bottom line should be considered.[5]

Schools should be places where people demonstrate the things they value. The values demonstrated in schools today tend to be impersonal, bureaucratic, and mechanistic, if not vapid. Getting the work done is important, getting good grades is important. What do teachers demonstrate about the point of education? What are the stories they tell?

THE NEED TO THINK

I have not provided easy answers for teachers, or for administrators. Teachers should not be told what to do; that would be the antithesis of the kind of thinking I have said should go on in schools. Teachers must use their own imagination in the classroom, not that of outside "experts." Teachers may argue about my conclusions; I hope they do, because I want them to argue with others.

All the topics raised in this book could be discussed with students—of any age. The issues are not complicated. Particular points of view should always take their chances, along with everything else in education; thinking should be demonstrated, not asserted. Thought must be trusted.

Not everyone can be a *great* thinker, relatively speaking. There will always be a range of individual differences in any human behavior. But we could all think *better*; we can all learn from better thinkers. What the world needs—I think—is not more great thinkers, but a greater amount and variety of commonplace thought about particular things. The stories that we all believe should be critically examined and creatively improved, and better alternatives should perhaps be offered to people who believe different stories.

Why do some cultures elevate the role of women and others demean it? Why do different groups take differing views on abortion, sex, child labor, material wealth, education, and respect for all people, for all animals, for the entire world? Economics or power may have been at the beginning of some or all of these attitudes, but they are perpetuated by stories. They are *believed*, and held to be natural and right, simply because they *make sense* to people; it is what they think.

The great problems of the world today—political, environmental, social, and economic—are not due to lack of facts, and probably not to lack of thought either. They reflect the *values* of people and governments, the stories they believe. There will be no solutions if we constantly wait for new skills and knowledge; what is required is an ability to recognize and understand the stories that are currently being played out, their consequences, and how they might be changed, in ourselves and others.

We each have a brain that can create and understand new realities. When people are reluctant to consider change, it is usually because they feel secure with the beliefs they have, not because they are ignorant. Because of the complexity of the world, it is often easier for people to reach agreement on what they are against rather than what they are for. The problem is not *how* people think—for which we would have to train a new generation—but *what* people think—for which we must openly examine ourselves.

Every generation holds the promise of a fresh start. The thinking and learning power of children is enormous. We have in our classrooms both the individuals and the imaginative possibilities required for the creation of better realities tomorrow. Our best hope is to provide environments where everyone is given the opportunity, support, and freedom—to think.

WHO'S RIGHT?

When I was invited to speak to a meeting of school administrators about some of the topics in this book, a very upset superintendent challenged me. He said that "another expert" had been in the district a couple of weeks earlier, and had taken quite a different position on thinking.

"He said one thing and you say another," said the superintendent. "How do you account for that?"

I suggested that at least one of us must be wrong.

He seemed taken aback by that possibility. "Then how do I find out who's right?" he asked.

His dilemma is obvious. He cannot ask experts to decide among themselves, and he cannot go to someone else for a judgment, because there is no guarantee that a third expert will be right. He will never get a guarantee that any expert is right.

It is ironic that an experienced and academically highly qualified leader of a school system, sincerely dedicated to helping his students "think better," should feel unable to think about the topic of thinking himself.

I suggested that he take his question back into his schools and discuss it with the teachers and students, not to find an "answer" but to accomplish what he wanted to achieve. He nodded his head. He may have been dissatisfied—but he was thinking.

NOTES

Acknowledgments

It is impossible to list sources for ideas contained in this book, but not because I want to claim all the credit for myself. The notion that "scholarly" writing can always be tied neatly into a network of other people's publications is academic fantasy. Real life is more complex. I have been influenced by many things that I have read, but a definitive list would have to go back to my youngest days and include a multitude of novels, biographies, histories, and newspaper and magazine articles as well as formal texts. I have been stimulated as much from disagreeing as from agreeing with the authors I have read. It is not difficult to find quotations to support any point of view, but nothing is proved by such selections. The same relativity applies to "research." It is too easy to find (or produce) experimental results or observations that support our prejudices, and to explain away (or suppress) the results that do not.

Many of the ideas in this book derive not from reading but from conversations and discussions I have had with colleagues, friends and opponents, once again regardless of unanimity or closure. Ideas are always more forthcoming when I am enjoying myself than when I am bored, so I have to acknowledge the special contribution of good company—in print or in person.

But I should not be reluctant to say that ideas in this book have also been considerably shaped by my own thinking—especially during the course of writing. Thinking is not rated highly in the rarified atmosphere of academia. *Introspection, armchair theorizing, hand-waving,* and *anecdotal* are among the pejorative terms used to characterize those who do not restrict their imagination to hypotheses tested in laboratories or simulated on computers, or who find much of such research uncompelling. Thought itself deserves some credit.

Two collaborators however must be named for their profound personal influence on this book. Without many long and congenial disputations with Bryant Fillion the book would never have been started, and without the insights and editing of Mary-Theresa Smith it would never have been finished.

135

Chapter 1: Talking About Thinking (pages 1–11)

1. It could be argued that the entire history of the study of thought has simply been the effort to find a satisfactory way of talking about it. For a long and significant period in the history of psychology, introspection was the *only* way to study thinking. The effort finally collapsed with demonstrations that thinking was frequently accomplished without observable "images" and in the absence of awareness on the part of the thinker. Subjects asked to relate what went on in their minds while they judged which of two weights was the heavier, for example, had nothing to report, no matter how long and intensely they reflected. One weight felt heavier than the other, and that was that. See Chapter 18 of Boring (1957), a classic history of experimental psychology that covers many of the efforts to study thought, and also Mandler & Mandler (1964).

Many philosophers have argued that thinking terms do not refer to mental events, including Wittgenstein (1958), Ryle (1949), and Quine (1960). See also Note 2 to Chapter 8. Wittgenstein claimed that "thinking" words do not refer to anything at all, but are simply moves in a "language game."

2. The word *skills* causes endless confusion in education. It is easily attached to mental activities (such as reading skills, writing skills, thinking skills, and problem-solving skills), conveying the assumption that improvement depends on instruction and exercises, as it does (to some extent) with physical skills. However, we do not have thinking skills in the same sense that we can have dancing skills or tennis skills. No muscular or motor coordination is involved. Thinking requires experience rather than practice; it improves with knowledge and authority, not with exercise. But even the words *practice* and *exercise* are ambiguous. To practice medicine is not the same as to practice scales on the piano, and to exercise authority is not the same as to exercise the thigh muscles. Thinking requires practice and exercise in the first sense, as an activity that is engaged in, but not in the second sense, as a contrived repetition of aspects of the whole.

Attneave (1974) discusses how knowledge, rather than skills, is the basis of comprehension.

3. For handbooks or summaries of the cognitive science approach to thinking, see Note 4, Chapter 7 below. Cognitive scientists in general assume there is so little difference between the ways humans and computers "think" (or "process information" or "organize knowledge") that computers can be programmed to engage in thoughtful activities like humans and used to simulate or test theories of human thought. Else-

where the idea is vehemently opposed. Searle (1984) proposes succinctly that "anything that calls itself 'science' probably isn't—for example, Christian science, or military science, and possibly even cognitive science or social science" (p. 11). He even rejects the notion that computers can "process information," since they have no "mental states" that resemble knowing or believing.

In a brief article entitled "If There Is Artificial Intelligence, Is There Such a Thing as Artificial Stupidity?" Liebowitz (1989) argues that computer-based "expert systems," such as those used by physicians, need to be told everything our common sense takes for granted, like the fact that an object cannot be in two places at once. Waldrop (1987) says that ordinary common sense is far too complex to teach to computers, involving as it does notions of causality, structure, processes, and time. Suchman (1987) argues that computers will not be able to talk to people until it is understood how people are able to talk to each other. Computers do not understand human language because they do not have and cannot understand intentions. Dreyfus & Dreyfus (1986) argue that computers will never produce "genuine" artificial intelligence, or even human professional expertise, because they lack intuition, the ability to switch from an actual situation to an imagined alternative. Penrose (1989) also argues at scholarly length that there are aspects of human thinking that can never be emulated by computers. For an imaginative—if not mind-boggling—survey of the directions some theorists believe human and computer intelligence might go in the future, see Moravec (1988). Among the possibilities he considers is the downloading of the entire contents of human brains into computers, which will then, of course, be able to think on our behalf.

In a conceptual (or semantic) switch, many cognitive scientists no longer talk about *thinking* (by humans or computers) but instead talk about the acquisition, organization, use, and retrieval of *knowledge* (by humans or computers). Computers have so far proved incapable of thinking or talking very convincingly because they largely lack knowledge of anything to talk and think about. A technical but relatively readable review of attempts to understand human knowledge is provided by Anderson (1989). He notes three basic theories and possible sources of knowledge, not necessarily exclusive—knowledge we are born with (nativism), knowledge we are given by our interactions with the environment (empiricism), and knowledge produced by our own reasoning (rationalism). Anderson describes the evolution of his own attempts to construct a theory of human knowledge, beginning with databases solely of "declarative knowledge" (facts), then adding "procedural knowledge" (rules), and, most recently, including knowledge related to functions or purposes. (It is interesting to compare this tripartite scheme with Tulving's three-level theory of memory, Note 1, Chapter 3 below, and Sternberg's triarchic theory of intelligence, Note 7, Chapter 2 below.) Significantly, in the light of arguments presented in Chapter 5 of this book, Anderson describes the acquisition and use of knowledge as essentially a matter of pattern-recognition, although his underlying metaphorical predilection is explicit in his observation that "in the 1960s and 1970s there appeared in cognitive psychology a set of theories [about human knowledge] that were sufficiently well-specified that they could be simulated on a computer" (p. 317).

There has also been a recent trend in cognitive science to replace the computer metaphor for how knowledge is organized with a brain metaphor, based on the actual physiological structure of neural networks within the skull ("wetware" rather than software). It is assumed that there are biological substrata, familiarly known as PDPs (parallel distributed processes), underlying every mental state. Comprehension is conceptualized in terms of the "spreading activation" or "transmission of activation levels" among dense networks of PDPs. Iran-Nejad (1989) describes the theoretical approach in an uncomplicated way and illustrates it with an experiment involving reader responses to stories with surprise endings. More technical discussion of these issues can be found in Fodor & Pylyshyn (1988) and in other articles in the same journal issue.

Chapter 2: Commonplace Thinking (pages 12–31)

1. For arguments that the brain is not very good at acquiring, using, and retrieving "information," see Smith (1983b, Chapter 13). It could be argued that contemporary thinking problems are due more to distraction and manipulation than to lack of information. In *More Die of Heartbreak*, Saul Bellow (1987) suggests that most of today's "information" is really "kitsch entertainment" in disguise.

2. Emotions are inseparable from all behavior and thinking. In an article boldly entitled "The Laws of Emotion," Frijda (1988) proposes that emotions arise predictably in response to the meaning of events to the individual, in other words, as a result of thinking. Emotions can be quite inconsistent. As a bizarre example, Herzog (1988) reveals that scientists can have contradictory—but apparently not conflicting—emotions about "good and bad" mice. Experimental mice in laboratories are protected and receive relatively considerate treatment. Intruders are treated as pests and can finish up in sticky traps known as "mice flypaper."

3. It could be argued that thinking is itself a construction of thought (see Note 4, Chapter 8 below). There is very little correlation between what we do and what we think we are doing. We think or use language without knowing what we know that enables us to think or use language. For the "tacit" nature of knowledge, see Polanyi (1958).

4. For detailed examples of specifications as intentions (in the case of writing) and as expectations (in the case of reading), see Smith (1983a).

5. Rock (1983) contends that perception is intelligent and based on operations similar to those that characterize thought. Nicholson (1984) argues that all perception is based on interpretation, which in turn is based on "empathy."

6. Deanna Kuhn (1989) criticizes the view that children (or untrained adults) literally think like scientists. Scientists distinguish theory and evidence, she claims, while children (and often adults) subtly adjust conflicting evidence or theory to bring them into alignment.

7. There is a multitude of books on the nature and improvement of thinking; two general ones are Gellatly (1986) and Gilhooly (1982). See also Note 4, Chapter 7 below.

An interesting example of an academic theory translated into a popular how-to manual is Sternberg (1988). He regards intelligence as "mental self-management" in three kinds of circumstances: (1) adapting to environments, (2) selecting new environments, and (3) shaping or modifying environments. He then spends the rest of his book demonstrating, through many homely examples and familiar puzzles, that ability to behave effectively in particular environments (such as taking intelligence tests) depends on understanding rather than databanks of facts or information. He criticizes intelligence tests for their content and consequences—but he is working on better ones.

For more technical expositions of Sternberg's research and theorizing into the nature of intelligence and thinking, without the helpful hints, see Sternberg (1983, 1985). Neisser (1983) criticizes Sternberg's efforts to reduce mental processes to components, quoting J. R. R. Tolkien—"He that breaks a thing to find out what it is has left the path of wisdom"—and arguing that things like "recognition of just what the nature of the problem is" and "understanding of internal and external feedback concerning the quality of task performance" are not separate elements in any genuine mental process but "more like chapter headings in books on how to think." Sternberg responds in the same journal issue.

8. Attempts to understand thinking in terms of the association of ideas (from British empiricist philosophers to present day behaviorists) have never succeeded in explaining anything because associations can be

found for every conceivable train of thought. The most common explanation for the establishment of associations, namely *frequency*, is clearly wrong. As a typical example, children are said to learn the meaning of *milk* by sheer repetition of hearing the word and seeing the referent together. But children frequently hear the word *milk* in the absence of the referent and see the referent without hearing or saying the word. What matters is the *purpose* for which the word is uttered. For the movement of the study of thought from mindless associations to intentional and purposeful *directed thinking* and *determining tendencies*, see Mandler & Mandler (1964).

9. Typically, what is called "good reasoning" is not logical thought but anything that can be defended against objections. And objections are usually based not on logic but on practical, pragmatic, or value considerations. Perkins (1985) says that reasoning is the construction of arguments to justify conclusions. Informal reasoning, he says, is not an impoverished or degraded version of formal reasoning; it is not "poor thinking." When informal reasoning leads to faulty conclusions, it is usually not through the commission of any error or fallacy of formal logic, but because sufficient or appropriate alternative possibilities are not taken into account, something that formal reasoning does not even claim to guard against.

Three centuries ago, Locke (1690/1924) also argued that the logical syllogism was "not the great instrument of reason . . . men, in their own enquiries after truth, never use syllogisms to convince themselves, because, before they can put them into a syllogism, they must see the connexion that is between the intermediate idea and the two other ideas it is set between and applied to, to show their agreement; and when they see that, they see whether the inference be good or no; and so syllogism comes too late to settle it" (Locke, 1690/1924, Book 4, Chapter 17). Habermas (1987) says that even philosophical discourse is literary rather than logical. There are only "local" logics, and what is logical depends on circumstances.

Henle (1962) presents experimental evidence that people usually think logically but change the premises to "answer a different question." Margolis (1987), on the other hand, thinks logic has nothing to do with thinking, which is based on "patterns" (see Note 3, Chapter 5 below). Johnson-Laird (1983) asserts that people do not naturally reason deductively but instead create and think about "mental models" of various possibilities.

Johnson & Blair (1985) review analyses of informal logic and attempt to make courses in logic more relevant to the contemporary world. They list dozens of different kinds of *fallacy* (from appeals to authority to equivocation and red herrings) as hazards to be watched for and shunned. Kahane (1976) also lists common fallacies, such as invalid arguments, questionable premises and evidence, distorted statistics, and emotive and misleading language. However, Finocchiaro (1981) argues that many alleged common fallacies are neither fallacious nor common; they are not usually a cause of defective thinking. Picking on fallacies can be an easy but unconstructive way to refute arguments.

10. The only specific attempt to distinguish lower- from higher-order thinking is the influential behavioristic "taxonomy" of Benjamin Bloom (1956), which places stimulus-response learning at the bottom of the theoretical hierarchy and the application and evaluation of that learning at the top, more valuable but more difficult. Designers of instructional programs and tests have used the taxonomy most, because it provides a rationale for sequencing tasks from easy to difficult. It has been argued that the taxonomy is irrelevant and even upside-down (Smith, 1986, Chapter 4) because it is based on experimental studies involving nonsense learning, by animals and by humans. In the real world it is easier to learn sense (where the application and value are obvious) than nonsense.

11. In experimental studies, Quinn (1987) observed that infants 3 and 4 months of age were able to categorize and conceptualize, without the benefit of language, even though almost everything in the experimental situation (and their lives) was a new experience. Children aged 4 years can anticipate the behavior of others based on false beliefs (Wimmer & Perner, 1983) and can reason perfectly well if logical aspects of tasks are embedded in meaningful contexts (Donaldson, 1978). Coles (1986a, 1986b) documents extensively that children have complex and sophisticated moral and political points of view that can be worth listening to by adults. Brown & Ferrara (1985) show that children perform and learn better if functioning (with assistance) at the upper levels of their potential. For other reviews of significant research on children's thinking, see Gelman (1979).

12. Cognitive scientists generally hold metacognition to be a special "executive" kind of thought, namely thought that is about thinking—see, for example, Bereiter & Scardamalia (1982) and Sternberg (1988). Alternatively, metacognition can be seen as a special kind of jargon for talking about assumed thinking processes. Like the "monitor" that Krashen (1985) hypothesizes as having a purely verbal function in language-learning, metacognitive knowledge enables us to talk about something without influencing how it is learned or done. In a typical review article on metacognitive research, Bransford, Stein, & Vye (1982) argue that less successful students fail to "activate knowledge"

that can help them to understand and remember "new information." But one might argue that "inability to activate knowledge" (which could be paraphrased less esoterically as "inability to make sense") is less a cause of failure than a description of the situation students find themselves in. The researchers also say that less successful students are less able to assess their own level of comprehension. But we all know when we are confused. If Bransford, Stein, & Vye instead mean that their subjects did not know that they were making mistakes, that is not a failure to stay in touch with one's own thought processes but a simple matter of being wrong and not knowing it, a not uncommon condition.

Chapter 3: Remembering, Understanding, and Learning (pages 32–44)

1. Tulving (1985a, b) distinguishes three aspects of memory, associated with three degrees of consciousness. *Procedural memory* is the most basic, consisting of learned connections or relationships among stimuli and responses, none of which is accessible to consciousness. Above this is *semantic memory*, or "knowledge," a specialized subsystem of procedural memory involving internal representations of states of the world not perceptually present, which we can be aware of not as events but as descriptions (we can describe a bird without having a particular bird in mind). Finally there is *episodic* memory, a specialized subsystem in semantic memory, which involves "self-knowing" of personally experienced events (actual or imagined) and temporal relationships (the sequence in which events occurred rather than actual dates). Bradburn, Rips, & Shevell (1987) have demonstrated how episodic memory usually takes precedence over the semantic. People have difficulty with autobiographical questions in surveys or questionnaires, tending to recall incidents as parts of coherent streams of events rather than as items of information. (They cannot remember the number of times they went to the dentist during a year, or the dates of the visits, but they do remember incidents.)

Experimental psychology has traditionally studied only procedural memory under contrived conditions—see Boring (1957). For an alternative "ecological" approach to memory, see an edited volume by Neisser & Winograd (1988); Brewer's chapter discusses research that sampled what subjects were thinking and remembering at randomly selected times during their daily lives. The results showed the importance of spatial location in memory, depending on the sense that is made of situations. In a classic demonstration, de Groot (1965) showed that chess masters could recall the positions of numerous pieces on the chess board in actual game situations but did no better than tyros when the pieces were randomly placed.

2. Extensive research by Carey (1978) led to the estimate that 6-year-olds have mastered (to some degree) an average of 14,000 words, mostly without formal instruction. M. Smith (1941) estimated third-grade children's vocabulary development at about 5,000 words a year, without (or despite) formal instruction. Nagy, Herman, & Anderson (1985) concluded that fifth-graders were learning an average of 4,875 new words a year, with a range of 1,500–8,250 words a year, depending mainly on the amount of reading done. High school students were still adding an average of about 3,000 new words a year to their vocabularies, mainly from reading. Elley (1989) reports New Zealand research showing how 7- and 8-year-old children make substantial vocabulary gains by listening to comprehensible and interesting stories, without any explanation of the unfamiliar words.

3. For the history of the experimental study of learning, see Boring (1957), and also Note 1, Chapter 1 above.

4. Piaget offers an alternative perspective. His views on learning, comprehension, and thinking (all of which he subsumed under the single heading of "adaptation") are broadly known, widely scattered, and not always accessible, physically or intellectually. For those not familiar with the subtle thought of Piaget, the best introduction is still probably Flavell (1963). For a more recent review of the continuing influence of Piaget in psychology and education, see Inhelder, de Caprona, & Cornu-Wells (1987). See also Note 5, Chapter 9 below. Vygotsky's (1978) view of learning in terms of "proximal development" is important—that what children can do with help today, they can (and probably will) do alone tomorrow.

Chapter 4: Imagination (pages 45–54)

1. Boulding (1981) asserts that human knowledge constitutes a unique and coherent world; it is not the interaction of a "real world" and a brain.

2. In massive documentation on dreams and a large variety of interpretations, the brain is almost invariably seen as trying to impose some kind of sense on what might otherwise be chaotic. Hobson (1988), for example, shares a contemporary theory that when "cognitive areas" of the forebrain are activated by essentially random neural events without sensory input or motor output, the ongoing activity is transformed

into a dream, in effect imposing some kind of meaning on what would otherwise be meaningless.

Play has also been widely documented and interpreted; one thing is clear, that it always make sense to the person playing. It is probably misleading to look for the "functions" or "purposes" of dreams or play. Play just *is*, a doing or being, rather than a tool or waystation toward something else. Gardner (1982) concludes that children know the difference between play and reality and can move easily from one to the other.

3. A number of recent psychological investigations have examined the manner in which imagery—in every sensory modality—facilitates comprehension, memory, and interest. The research is briefly summarized in Long, Winograd, & Bridge (1989). They showed that fifth-grade students spontaneously produced mental imagery, whether they were reading poems, stories, or expository texts, and that the students' interest in what they read increased with the amount of imagery they reported. For technical contributions and reviews on the topic of imagery and thought see Kosslyn (1980, 1983), Paivio (1986), and Sheikh (1983). The imagery involved in the pervasiveness of metaphor in language and thought has also attracted attention; see, for example, Ortony (1979). See Walkerdine (1982) for the centrality of metaphor in children's thought and learning, and also J. Miller (1983).

Wong (1980) showed that the use of questions and prompts (to stimulate the imagination) enhanced the comprehension and retention of implied information in "learning-disabled" children, raising their ability to make inferences to that displayed by good readers; see also Hansen (1981). Levin, Shriberg, & Berry (1983) found that eighth-grade students had better recall of short abstract prose passages when they were illustrated by one complex picture than by four simple ones of separate components of the story.

The same pathways in the brain are stimulated by imagining as by actually engaging in any physical or mental activity (Waitley, 1983). *Visualization* of a desired outcome is often a component of improved and exceptional performance.

4. The Perkins article is discussed in Note 9, Chapter 2.

5. Bruner has made important and lucid contributions on the dependence of perception on knowledge and expectation (Bruner, 1973), on categorical aspects of thinking (Bruner, Goodenow, & Austin, 1956), and on the creative and narrative nature of thought (Bruner, 1986). See also Bruner & Haste (1987).

6. For a historical analysis of wondering as a classical art, see Covino (1988). For a general, popular, and idiosyncratic account of "the

origins of knowledge and imagination," see Bronowski (1978). Berthoff (1983) writes eruditely on "reclaiming the imagination."

Chapter 5: Patterns and Stories (pages 55–71)

1. For a more complete analysis of theories of letter, word, and speech recognition, see Smith (1988b, Chapters 6 and 7).
2. We strive to impose order even on random arrangements of numbers and letters (Klahr, Chase, & Lovelace, 1983; Restle, 1971). Dasser, Ulbaek, & Premack (1989) demonstrate that preschool children spontaneously attribute both causality and intentionality to images of two balls moving on a blank screen—they are seen to "fall over a cliff," "struggle to get back up," and even to "help each other."
3. Margolis (1987) argues at length that all thinking and judgment can be reduced to pattern-recognition, noting that "what people believe is only weakly correlated with a reasonable assessment of the objective logic of a situation" (1987, p. ix). He regards the brain as "a-logical, a-rational" rather than illogical and irrational, seeing "habits of mind" as fluent automatic prompting of patterns from context. He talks of spirals of "pattern cognitions" going from context to context, the pattern that one context suggests becoming part of the context for the next pattern. We often appear to think logically when we do not, and we can give equally confident reasons for false propositions as for true. "Faulty" thinking is regular thinking that happens to lead to faulty or unacceptable conclusions.

In lengthy speculation about the evolution of thinking, Margolis sees the brain settling for pattern-recognition rather than information processing as a tradeoff between deciding too soon and hesitating too long. We can operate in more than one pattern at a time, or switch between patterns rapidly, provided they are in different contexts (such as scientists who research in Einsteinian physics but teach in Newtonian). Polanyi's (1958) "tacit knowledge" is often tacit blindness—we "know" what to ignore, including gaps in arguments. "Illusions of thinking"—such as Kahneman, Slovic, & Tversky's (1982) demonstrations that thinking frequently ignores actual probabilities—are simply "scenario effects," responses to the pattern of particular contexts and habits of mind. Other Margolis assertions: Problem-solving is accomplished by "internal simulation"; reasoning is a "specialized form of judgment that is built out of pattern recognition applied to forms of language" (p. 56); intuition is "broad" and "loose" thinking; formal logic and mathematics are special "refined" kinds of language; and logical thinking ("patterns of reasoning-why") is a "learned knack," like chess and concert music. Logical thinking is something we can learn to do (like violin playing), but it is not built into the brain. The same applies to language. We do not believe something just because it is logical, any more than we believe an illusion just because we see it.

For a technical discussion of how humans (and computers) might handle knowledge and make decisions by pattern-recognition rather than reasoning, see Frey (1986). He combines a computer concept of "bit-mapped classifiers," which essentially detect the presence or absence of critical features, with a psychological theory that "natural categories" of experience do not have fixed boundaries but rather central and peripheral attributes (as a result of which, for example, some birds, such as robins, are considered more "birdlike" than other birds, such as penguins and pelicans). The psychological theory, propounded mainly by Eleanor Rosch (see Rosch & Lloyd, 1978), has also influenced a psychological-linguistic theory that the meanings imposed on the world are based on bodily metaphors (see Note 3, Chapter 8 below). Frey argues that doctors and detectives do not reason by deduction, but rather gather evidence that will confirm or disconfirm the most likely hypotheses about attributes of "prime suspects." "Knowing which attributes to include separates an expert from a novice," says Frey. He claims that the classifier approach is a model of organizational simplicity compared with structured knowledge and progressive reasoning, more in keeping with the cyto-architecture of the brain than knowledge networks.

Elsewhere, Stillings and colleagues (1987) theorize that neuroscience research may ultimately tell us why "the physical design of nervous systems is good for parallel pattern recognition and bad for serial tree-searching computations" (p. 266). For problem-solving as pattern-recognition, see Mandler (1984).

4. The English word *schemes* has become the standard term for various conceptualizations of abstract mental patterns that enable us to impose meaningfulness on regular occurrences in the world, although designation of the area of study—*schema theory*—continues to perpetuate the Latin term introduced by Bartlett (1932). In a comprehensive review of the topic, Mandler (1984) distinguishes three broad categories of schemes: *scenes*, or spatially organized knowledge; *events* (or *scenarios* and *scripts*); and *stories*. Since relationships among people play a prominent role in most scenes and events, the entire area could as well be called *story theory*.

Habits are embedded in scenarios. The first rules for breaking habits are (1) see yourself as a different kind of person and (2) avoid the situations in which the habits are most likely to control behavior. Even Pavlovian conditioning in animals has been found to be inseparable from meaning and interpretation. Rescorla (1988) reports that after many failures of the original experimental paradigm, conditioning is no longer regarded as the acquired ability of one stimulus to evoke the original response to another, but now involves learning relations among events "to allow the organism to represent its environment."

5. The universal elements of stories are necessarily identical with universal elements perceived in the world, including characters, situations, events, conflicts, problems, challenges and quests, motives, intentions, hopes and fears, and outcomes, resolutions, and endings. Characters may be good or evil, strong or weak, happy or sad, humble or arrogant, successful or unsuccessful—all of the ways in which the world and events in it are perceived. We are frequently characters in our own stories, and we identify with characters in other stories, which thus become our stories. The essential elements of stories are built into the structure of language—in the subject, verb, and object of traditional and transformational grammars and in the "case" relationships of semantic grammars.

Attempts to explain story comprehension are necessarily circular. We all must have a "story grammar" in our head. What is the grammar like? The structure of stories. The same applies to attempts to explain "procedural knowledge." How do we know what to do when we enter a restaurant? Answer—we have a "script" in our head for entering restaurants. What is the script like? Like what we do when we enter restaurants. We always finish up with a description of the phenomenon we are attempting to explain. Novelists can disclose as much about the nature of people as psychologists and sociologists, not because writers occasionally behave "scientifically" or "systematically," but because psychologists and sociologists can only see the world in the same fundamental terms as novelists, no matter how much they envelop their research in esoteric techniques and abstruse jargon.

Theories that claim to cover everything are conventionally believed to explain nothing. It might be asked what difference regarding the brain as a storytelling device could make. But metaphors control the way we view the world. The alternative metaphors for the brain—that it is an information-processing device, a computer, an empty vessel, a habit-forming stimulus-response mechanism, or a reservoir of unconscious desires and conflicts—are different ways of looking at the world and have different consequences. One area in which the brain metaphor makes an enormous difference is education, influencing perceptions of how children develop as thinkers and therefore how they should be taught.

6. Nelson (1986) and many collaborators describe how children organize and recount experience in terms of "events," not of specific

episodes but of what typically occurs or might be expected or wished to occur. They think in narrative form. Sulzby (1985) shows that kindergarten children always make sense of their early reading attempts by telling (or making up) a meaningful story, and van Dongen (1987) outlines how children's thought continually runs on narrative lines at home and at school. For a discussion of the imaginativeness of children and of "teaching as story telling," see Egan (1989). Vygotsky (1978) says that children's memories begin as internalized narratives that, over time, become related to everything else they know about the world, their broader stories, involving causes, purposes, and consequences. Langer (1951) offers subtle and profound arguments that experience of a story is no different from experience of "actual events."

7. Boorstin (1985) paints a broad picture of the constant struggle of every society to convert others to its stories, committing any crime to substantiate its own stories (if the crime is permitted by the stories).

Joseph Campbell and Northrop Frye have extensively documented the pervasiveness of mythic themes throughout all the cultures of the world—for example, Campbell (1949) and Frye (1963). For the timeless appeal of the Ulysses theme, see Stanford (1968).

8. In an edited volume, L. Smith (1988) surveys the educational influence of Anne E. Berthoff's view of the meaning-making creativeness of all human thought (see Berthoff, 1981). Among several chapters focusing on storytelling as a mode of knowing, Knoblauch & Brannon (1988) note that "Bohr and Heisenberg are acutely aware of the narrator of physics, the 'story'-teller who produces the data and interprets it according to the rules of that art in order to produce a coherent text."

Barbara Hardy—in Meek, Warlow, & Barton (1977)—argues that narrative is a primary act of mind, and Moffett (1968) proposes that narrative must "do for all." For "the importance of story," see an article with that title by Rosen (1986, also 1988), and also Bateson (1980). Postman (1989) says that individuals and nations may die for lack of believable stories. For a classic description of how stories and descriptions have always been the basis of memory systems, especially before the advent of writing, see Yates (1966).

Chapter 6: Thinking Creatively (pages 72–90)

1. Howard Gardner (1982) and David Perkins (1981) were co-directors of Harvard University's *Project Zero* study of artistic thinking. Both view creativity as "the mind's best work." Gardner is dazzled by the achievement of "masters" like Mozart, Darwin, and Freud. He is most concerned with the general notion that brains function according

to "rules" and "symbols," although what is interesting about the brain is not the fact that it uses symbols to represent worlds (a debatable proposition) but that it creates worlds that include symbols. In a subsequent book, Gardner (1983) outlines a "theory of multiple intelligences," arguing that we all have at least seven independent "intelligences"—linguistic, musical, logical-mathematical, spatial, bodily-kinesthetic, and two kinds of "personal." Gardner is presumably speaking metaphorically— we behave *as if* we have these different intelligences, and differ from each other in terms of our abilities and preferences along these directions (and along many others as well).

Perkins (1981) argues that geniuses do not think differently from other people; they tend to know more facts and have a greater repertoire of operations in the areas in which they are geniuses, like mathematicians who can make lightning calculations. The book is a good source for many stories about insight, intuition, and inspiration. He concludes that creative thinking is selective, governed by intention, making use of accident, and aided by planning and flexibility. For a fuller review of these books, see Smith (1985) in a journal issue devoted to creativity, thinking, and education.

In contrast to Gardner and also to Sternberg (see Note 7 to Chapter 2 above), Howe (1988) argues that the word *intelligence* explains nothing; it simply means that a person will do well on certain kinds of task. Like the term *productivity*, Howe asserts, *intelligence* simply rephrases what is already known.

2. In a noteworthy series of studies, MacKinnon (1962) compared highly creative with less creative architects (as identified by their peers). The highly creative architects tended to describe themselves as inventive, independent, industrious, and individualistic. Their less creative colleagues were more inclined to see themselves as virtuous, of good character, rational, and sympathetically concerned for others. The more creative architects were not necessarily more intelligent, but they were more intuitive, more open to experience, and not preoccupied with the impression they made. They were also more sensitive, more open to their own feelings and emotions, and had wide-ranging interests—characteristics that earned them high ratings on the femininity scale of the MMPI (Minnesota Multiphasic Personality Inventory) test battery, a result that probably says more about definitions of femininity than about architects. MacKinnon notes that the parents of creative architects usually had "extraordinary respect" for their children and confidence in their ability to do what was appropriate.

Similar findings are reported in a study of scientific geniuses like Einstein, Pasteur, and Darwin by Simonton (1988), who notes especially his subjects' enthusiasm, industriousness, and "immense productivity." He also emphasizes the role of chance in establishing circumstances in which a particular genius might flower or be forever unrealized: A cobbler might have the capacity to be a great general, if only he could be a general. Simonton also notes that geniuses allow chance, in the form of accidents, imagery, and play, to dominate creative aspects of their thinking. A similar point is made by Cameron (1960), who argues that variation in creative thinking (and in evolution itself) must be *blind;* it cannot be bound by current circumstances.

3. Children are often told in effect that they are not creative, and they learn exactly what is demonstrated to them. Gardner (1982) has several hypotheses about why the richness of children's creativeness may fade, noting that they develop a desire for conformity, self-consciouness, and even a fascination with "reality" and its mastery that may make them become more literal.

Chapter 7: Thinking Critically (pages 91–107)

1. Margolis (1987) claims to have resolved the "belief/knowledge" conundrum as part of his theory of thinking as pattern-recognition (see Note 3 to Chapter 5 above). He distinguishes two dimensions to belief— one of gestalt *intuition* (abbreviated as I and characterized as "does the *result* look right?") and another of *critical* analysis (abbreviated as C and characterized as "does the *argument* look right?"). Positive responses to both I and C result in knowledge, says Margolis. Positive I and neutral C equal belief, and neutral I and negative C equal doubt. Among the other permutations, positive I and negative C equal paradox.

2. One might ask whether the subjects in the celebrated experiments of Milgram (1974) lacked essential thinking skills. Acting as "teachers," they continued to increase to lethal levels the voltage of electric shocks delivered (so they thought) to poorly achieving "learners" when assured by authority—in this case the experimental psychologist—that it was their job to do so.

3. D'Angelo (1971) lists ten "attitudes" necessary for critical thinking: intellectual curiosity, objectivity, open-mindedness, flexibility, intellectual scepticism, intellectual honesty, being systematic, persistence, decisiveness, and respect for other viewpoints.

People can persist in unproductive behavior, even when it is apparent that costs and losses are escalating. Staw & Ross (1989) show how individuals may refuse to believe that they are embarked on a mistaken course of action or that further investment will not turn their fortunes around. They can also be reluctant to admit errors to others, especially where security and support are low. The structure of organizations may make it more difficult (in effect, less rational) to admit unproductive courses of behavior.

Shannon & Fernie (1985) argue against the popular sentiment that literacy is superior to television watching in developing and exercising critical thought. Print and television can be used as complementary tools to "help children develop into thoughtful citizens who can critically examine and understand the world."

4. Many books on the topics of teaching or improving thinking claim to be based on the latest insights of cognitive science. An interesting example is Bransford & Stein (1984), whose all-embracing title is *The IDEAL Problem Solver: A Guide for Improving Thinking, Learning and Creativity*. IDEAL is an acronym for the problem-solving system they propose: *I*dentify problem; *D*efine and represent problem; *E*xplore possible strategies; *A*ct on the strategies; and *L*ook back and evaluate the effects of your strategies. It might be asked whether such a procedure could help anyone who did not understand the problem they confronted in the first place, or would be necessary for anyone who did understand the problem. The authors claim that their system is "solidly grounded" in basic research in areas such as cognitive psychology, education, philosophy and artificial intelligence. The idea that artificial intelligence studies can help people to learn and think is common among cognitive scientists. In a volume entitled *Reading and Understanding: Teaching from the Perspective of Artificial Intelligence*, Schank (1982) draws comparisons between teaching reading to his daughter and to a computer.

Hitchcock (1983) recommends the OMSITOG approach. The acronym in this case is a puzzle in itself, standing for: get *O*verview of passage; clarify *M*eaning; portray *S*tructure of argumentation, if any; check whether *I*nferences are sound; evaluate *T*ruth of claims not supported by argument; consider *O*ther relevant evidence and arguments; and *G*rade the passage.

Two volumes of perspectives on teaching thinking—Segal, Chipman, & Glaser (1985) and Chipman, Segal, & Glaser (1985)—include chapters by such influential figures as de Bono and Feuerstein, who should be read critically. Despite their widely divergent approaches, most authors in both volumes have no doubt about the particular assumptions from which they proceed or the conclusions that they reach. Almost evangelically at times, they see teaching thinking as possible, desirable, and, if their own method is followed, inevitable. They are rarely explicit about the theory of thinking or learning that underlies their point of view. In the second volume, Brown (1985) demonstrates that cognitive science approaches to teaching children to think are essentially no different from pioneer test constructor Alfred Binet's "mental orthopedics" program for teaching children in the early 1900s. For an overview of traditional approaches to "improving thinking skills," see Halpern (1984). Popular contemporary approaches to teaching "thinking skills" fall into three general categories: the "metacognitive" strategy of making students more aware of their "thinking processes" (see Note 12, Chapter 2 above); a mental agility method of exercising the mind through problems and puzzles (de Bono, 1976); and a pedagogic approach based on teacher questioning intended to stimulate thinking directly (Beyer, 1983).

In some critical thinking about de Bono and Feuerstein, Wong (1989) draws a distinction between teaching children strategies (which she concedes some instructional programs might do) and teaching them to be strategic. She thinks the instructional programs ignore individual differences and fail to check for generalization and maintenance of what might be taught. Sternberg & Bhana (1986) also criticize influential theories of intellectual skills training, from their own point of view.

For a history of the "critical-thinking movement" in American education, see Paul (1985), in a journal issue devoted to critical thinking. Despite "nearly 400 years of 'miseducation,'" Paul argues that it is still possible to teach critical thinking. In a review of efforts in the 1930s and 1960s to teach reasoning, Cuban (1984a) describes the difficulties that the social situation in many classrooms imposes on teachers and students in exercising critical thought. He credits (or blames) John Dewey (1910) for the idea that good thinking is essentially scientific reasoning—problem identification, data collection, and hypothesis testing. For a history of what can go wrong with programs or policies to teach thinking in schools, see Cuban (1984b). In an interesting and unusual book, McPeck (1990) reflects on his earlier volume (1981) and includes some contrary points of view.

From a behavioristic perspective, Herrnstein, Nickerson, de Sanchez, & Swets (1986) trained elementary school children on specific intelligence-test kinds of task (analyzing similarities and differences) and reported that IQ test scores improved. However, Lehman, Lempert, & Nisbett (1988) review a number of studies of the effect of graduate training on reasoning and conclude that "learning how to solve one problem produces no improvement in solving others having an identical formal structure," although formal training in particular areas, such as medicine, psychology, chemistry, and law, improves "pragmatic inferential" thought.

Chapter 8: Thinking and Language (pages 108-123)

1. Mary-Theresa Smith (personal communication) suggests that it makes as much sense to talk about the functions of thought or language as it would to talk about the functions of electricity or air. All can be used for a variety of purposes, doubtless including many still to be discovered.

Konner (1982) and Lenneberg (1967) argue that language must have a biological basis because it makes its appearance in all infants at about the same age, independently of the behavior of their parents and of the particular language that they will learn (including sign languages). Like Lenneberg before him, Konner destroys much of the case for the uniqueness of language in humans with accounts of the enormous efforts to teach language to other primates, not without superficial success. Chimpanzees and gorillas have learned vocabularies of hundreds of words and many grammatical rules and demonstrated that they could use them, sometimes in novel conditions. Everything would seem set for these animals to take off with their new language ability, but they never seem to comprehend what can be *done* with language; they use their competence minimally. The simple reason why only humans have exploited language, I suspect, is that other creatures do not have very much to talk about. They may live in what looks to us like a rich and interesting environment, but imagination is not something they appear to project upon it.

By contrast, Konner himself tells of a 10-month-old child who constantly pointed at things and said "Dat"—"questioningly or indicatively or emphatically or thoughtfully . . . she seems to be announcing the existence of a relationship between a piece of the great world and her own presumptive mind, a relationship that has evidently surprised her. . . . I suspect that what we are looking at is the most rudimentary form of what may be the key to being human; a sort of wonderment at the spectacle of the world, and its apprehensibility by the mind" (p. 172). In other words, imagination.

2. Illich & Sanders (1988) warn of the dangers of reducing language to a communication code—and "the degradation that results from the fallout of scientific discourse into ordinary speech" (p. 107). They choose as an example the word *energy,* which 400 years ago meant "vigor of expression" (in speech and in organ music), then in the nineteenth century became a technical term to denote the body's ability to perform work, and finally in physics to refer to increasingly abstract alternative forms of "energy" and to "energy needs." Illich & Sanders remark: "We must be forever conscious of the fact that we do not know

what those terms mean. . . . Furthermore, we gratefully transfer the power to define their meaning to an expertocratic hierarchy to which we do not belong. The word 'energy' in this context is used neither with common sense, nor with the senseless precision of science, but almost like a sublinguistic grunt, a nonsense word" (p. 106). The list of terms Illich & Sanders add as examples of sublinguistic grunts includes *sexuality, transportation, crisis, role,* and several words particularly relevant to the concerns of the present book: *education, communication, information, problem,* and *solution.*

3. In a book provocatively entitled *Women, Fire, and Dangerous Things* (which happen to be juxtaposed in an Australian aboriginal linguistic category), Lakoff (1987) rejects the "classical" view that categories (and truth) exist in the world and that language reflects the world. He argues instead that categories (and language) reflect our experience of the world and are constructed out of metaphors related to the human body, its activities and concerns, a theory he terms *experiential realism* or *experientialism.*

The need for shared understanding to overcome problems of vagueness and ambiguity in language, whatever the topic of discussion, has been pointed up experimentally by Garrod & Anderson (1987). They noted that in specific situations (such as playing a maze game) pairs of speakers adopt very similar forms of description depending as much on "local" semantic considerations (specific to the task at hand) as to general semantic knowledge. Speakers negotiate these common "mental models" spontaneously in order to have mutually comprehensible discussions, and they are not helped by imposed solutions.

Language does not simply describe things; it determines how they are seen. Language is power, and history determines meanings through social experience. Arguments like these are discussed from the point of view of gender theory in Hare-Mustin & Marecek (1988). They also provide a convenient summary of postmodernist theories like *constructivism* (that experience constructs reality, and the "real nature" of differences—for example, between genders—can never be determined) and *deconstructionism* (that meanings in excess of the author's intentions exist in every text and can be "deconstructed" to reveal webs of unintended meanings).

While widely speculated upon elsewhere, the role of wit and humor in language and thought has been largely ignored in the theorizing of cognitive psychologists and scientists. A major reason for verbal humor may be to establish, maintain, and monitor common ground among participants in language use, according to a readable (and mildly amusing) attempt to establish a taxonomic theory of humor in a cognitive science context by Long & Graesser (1988).

4. In order to doubt, one must assume that the world is not always what it seems or is said to be. We must recognize the existence in ourselves and others of "mental states" that do not necessarily reflect the world or behavior. Olson (Olson & Babu, 1989) says that critical thinking is discourse about talk and thought, concerned with beliefs, inferences, assumptions, and other "mental state" terms. These states are not usually marked in language—school science texts do not distinguish inferences, assumptions, and beliefs from statements of fact. Since it is difficult to reflect on what someone else has said in the absence of written record, critical thought is essentially synonymous with literacy; once the conceptual tools for the criticism of texts have been acquired, the criticism of everything else follows (see Note 6 below).

Olson (1989), Pylyshyn (1984), Fodor (1978), and Searle (1983) all argue on various grounds that "the mind" has no objective status but is constructed of mental states—such as perceptions, beliefs, and intentions—encouraged by culture. Children, lower animals, and computers cannot think because they do not entertain beliefs and doubts. Naturally, there is an opposing point of view, that beliefs and intentions as well as minds are fictions; we only think we have them—Quine (1960), Ryle (1949).

5. For performative uses of language, see Searle (1983).

6. Vygotsky (1962, 1978) presents an extreme view that internalized language *is* the basis of thought, "inner speech" being a transition from the external control of infant behavior by the language of others to personal control by the internalized language of oneself.

7. For typical arguments that literacy has made significant differences to the way we all think, see Stock (1983) and Ong (1977). Olson, Torrance, & Hildyard (1985) is an edited overview with several significant contributions. Among dissenters, Scribner & Cole (1981) offer comparative evidence that reading and writing may enable people to do different things, but not to think better. In a summary review of the history and semiotics of writing systems, Watt (1989) explores the notion that whatever written languages have in common, despite their enormous diversity, probably reflects the nature of thought itself. He discusses arguments that written language is related directly to thought rather than to spoken language. For the relationship of writing and the bureaucratic mind, see Innis (1951).

In an intriguingly idiosyncratic book, LePan (1989) argues that roughly until Shakespeare's time few people had mental states such as expectations. Actions were not related to intentions, and belief (as in belief in God) meant "trust" rather than credence. The future was ordained, "looked for" rather than anticipated, and no distinction was drawn between natural and supernatural causes. From his analyses of history, literature, drama, and anthropology, LePan concludes that new ways of thinking developed between the twelfth and mid-seventeenth centuries. (He does not speculate why this should be the case; Olson would attribute it to literacy.) The ability to form expectations is not an independent psychological faculty, according to LePan, but rather a byproduct of the ability to engage in certain sorts of causal and temporal thought. He conjectures that the thought of the bulk of the medieval population might have more in common with the thought of children than with that of modern Western adults.

8. The phenomenon of renowned experts and their followers colliding in total and belligerent disagreement can be examined in Piattelli-Palmarini's (1980) account of a debate between Noam Chomsky and Jean Piaget. Scarcely any issue was settled, although many important questions were raised about relationships among language, thought, and the world. This was not a matter of complementary points of view—at least one of the major protagonists has to be wrong, and they both labored mightily to prove it was the other.

For another vigorous critique of Chomsky's notions of the relationship of language, thinking, and behavior, see Robinson (1975). He argues that language is not explained by reduction to a different language or to different words—a mistaken notion that (to give an example of Robinson's) "paraphrase into relative clauses is somehow an achievement of a new kind of clarity or that 'cause + become + not + alive' is somehow explanatory of 'kill'" (p. xi). This book is an excellent demonstration of how a prestigious authority can be systematically taken apart by someone who persistently asks, "What has this got to do with the way people actually think and behave?"

Johnson-Laird, Hermann, & Chaffin (1984) critically examine the assumption that "meaning" can be represented by networks of labeled connections, arguing that meaning connects words to the world, not to other words.

Chomskyian transformational grammar has been criticized for being too focused on rules of syntax at the expense of the reason language is produced (and understood) on any particular occasion. Led by Halliday (1973), a vigorous field of systemic-functional linguistics has developed, emphasizing the social functions that language fulfills and the situations in which it occurs (and from which it is always inseparable).

See Butler (1989) and other articles in the same journal issue for technical surveys and summaries of the current state of systemic linguistics.

9. For more on talking to oneself, see Smith (1983b, Chapter 10).
People who say they can think only in words, or in visual images, are not
really talking about thinking. It would be better to say they *imagine* (or
have mental images) only in words or pictures. The thinking that underlies all imagery occurs neither in words nor in pictures; it produces the
images. But it is also not correct to assert that particular individuals can
think or learn only in auditory or visual images. Everyone who sees
must be capable of producing visual images, and everyone who talks
must be capable of hearing others speaking in their "mind's ear." We all
have preferences and propensities for thinking (or imagining) in particular ways, not because we have different kinds of brain, or lack particular
kinds of skill, but because we are all different. Some people go to concerts, others to art galleries; some prefer ballets to symphonies, others
have the opposite preference, and still others choose opera over either.
The differences speak to experience and inclination, not to particular
neural connections (see also the following note).

10. Popular theories of brain function talk of specific areas of the
brain being "responsible" for particular cognitive skills, of hemispheric
specialization, and of visual or auditory "learning styles." Simplistic
statements of this kind are usually made by psychologists or educators
who understand little of the complexity of neurophysiology or by
neuroscientists who understand little of the complexity of behavior and
learning. Scientific studies of the architecture and functioning of the
brain show enormous intricacy and interrelatedness in the organization
of the human brain. Gazzaniga (1989), in a summary article, reports
that there is specificity in the corpus callosum, connecting the two
hemispheres of the brain, on the *input* side only, for incoming visual and
auditory "information," for example. Within the hemispheres of the
brain there are no separate and isolated skills or functions; each hemi-
sphere contributes to the other. When the two sides are separated (by
callosal section), neither side functions normally. The interaction of
neural structures in many areas of the brain is essential for cognitive
activities; the brain functions as a whole.

The U.S. Army has apparently invested heavily in technologies to
improve learning and thinking based on brain research. In a summary
article, Holden (1987) reports that several hundred generals received
training in "neurolinguistic programming," based on the idea that individuals have different visual, auditory, or kinesthetic learning styles.
However, a committee of the National Research Council, which evalu-

ated the enterprise, found no scientific evidence of effective results. Nor did the committee find any value when material was selectively presented to the two hemispheres of the brain in accordance with hemispheric dominance theories.

Education has had a long connection with the military. Much research into learning and thinking, especially by cognitive scientists, is supported by the armed services (Noble, 1989). Militaristic language has come to pervade education: *task forces* are *recruited* to identify *targets* and *objectives*; *strategies* and *tactics* are devised to attain them, supported by *batteries* of tests. Students are *reinforced* for learning word *attack* skills and *promoted* or *withdrawn* depending on the *advances* they make. Of course, these are "only metaphors," but the words we use color and reflect the way we think. We could use meteorological or agricultural metaphors more extensively in education, the way we do in everyday life, with stormy debates and fertile minds, but about the only common one in education is *growth*.

11. Vygotsky (1978) emphasizes the social nature of thought, which he sees as internalized action and language (see Note 6 above): "Every function in the child's cultural development appears twice; first on the social level, and later, on the individual level" (p. 57). All "higher" functions like memory, attention, and perception, he argues, develop from actual relations among people that become internalized; "for the young child, to think means to recall; but for the adolescent, to recall means to think" (p. 51).

For the behavior of crowds, and for an analysis of power generally, see Canetti (1973).

12. McGinn (1989) proposes that the "mind-body problem" will never be solved, for the simple reason that we do not have the kind of mind (or brain) that would recognize the solution if it stared us in the face. Consciousness, which he sees as the "hard nut" of the problem, is accessible only to introspection and cannot be conceptualized spatially, while the perceptual systems that we would use to inspect the brain are geared only to representing a world of space and motion. Ironically, what makes us good at science precludes understanding the link between consciousness and the brain.

Chapter 9: Thinking and Education (pages 124–133)

1. The reasons many minority groups experience persistent school failure are considered by Cummins (1989). He argues that educational programs that develop in minority students a strong sense of confidence in themselves and their ability to learn almost invariably succeed—even

though "the educators who have initiated and taught in these programs [have had to] defend them against reactions ranging from skepticism to overt racism" (p. viii). For an ethnographic analysis of the classroom as a cultural institution, uncovering how students "learn to be a student" and "learn to do school," see Bloome, Puro, & Theodorou (1989).

In an article entitled "Why Johnny Can't Think: The Politics of Bad Schooling," social critic Walter Karp (1985) analyzes what he calls "the tyranny of the short right answer." Goodlad (1984) observed a thousand U.S. classrooms and found students spending only 1 percent of their time doing anything more complicated than recalling facts they were supposed to have learned. Wendler, Samuels, & Moore (1989) note that teachers asked to pay special attention to "teaching comprehension" simply asked more questions.

2. Children learn to write the way they do from what they read— without the benefit of instruction, and not always to their own good. Calkins (1980) found that children learned more about punctuation from their reading than from instruction, and Eckhoff (1983) reports that children whose writing consisted of a few short sentences, each on a separate line, had been reading exactly the same kind of "story" in their reading primers. Children whose reading was more conventional wrote in more conventional ways. Stanovich & West (1989) and Nagy, Herman, & Anderson (1985) describe how students who read more learn more about reading.

Tierney, Soter, O'Flahavan, & McGinley (1989) report that undergraduate students think more critically when engaged in combined reading and writing tasks than when reading alone, writing alone, answering questions, or engaging in some other pedagogical strategy designed to promote thinking. In other words, thinking is promoted when reading and writing have a purpose rather than being done as an academic exercise. See also Greene (1988) for the importance of the language arts in supporting thinking and the organization of experience.

3. Berthoff (1984) argues that many college students have difficulty with argumentation because the persuasion they breathe is advertisement. Novelist Josef Skvorecky (1977), in *The Engineer of Human Souls*, questions whether people are free to think if their thinking is done for them. Doris Lessing (1986) wants children to be told they will have to live in a world full of mass movements, deluged with ideas and opinions that are mass produced, and pressured all through their life, often by their closest friends, to join or conform to mass movements (pp. 73–74).

4. For a discussion of power relations in classrooms, see Giroux

(1988) and Walkerdine (1985). For arguments that the way children are taught establishes and perpetuates class distinctions, see Roller (1989) and Shannon (1985).

Heath (1985) argues that students cannot become or remain literate without opportunities to talk (and think) about literate matters. She emphasizes the central role of individual teachers in enabling students from a variety of backgrounds to succeed in and outside school. McLeod (1986) examines how students and teachers can take control of their own classrooms, and Shannon (1989) discusses ways to control and use literacy critically. For authoritative critiques of education, with many suggestions about better ways of helping children to learn, see Holt (1976, 1989).

The autonomy of teachers is limited by many influences outside the classroom (not always visible), and by the daily school routine to which teachers themselves must defer. A powerful source of authority in classrooms is the school text, which is "beyond criticism," according to an important analysis by Luke, de Castell, & Luke (1983).

There have been widespread calls for an *ethnographic* approach to educational research, employing nonintrusive anthropological techniques of observation and interpretation, especially in relation to literacy. See Spindler (1982) for descriptions of the techniques; Goelman, Oberg, & Smith (1984) for many illustrations of the approach in relation to early literacy; and Heath (1983) for a classic in the genre. A readable outline of *hermeneutics*, the philosophical discipline on which theories of interpretation are based, is Palmer (1969), and more recently and comprehensively Eagleton (1983). For an influential scholarly contribution, see Gadamer (1975).

Spindler (1974) is a primer for an anthropological approach to education. The tone of the volume is indicated by the title of a provocative chapter by McDermott (1974), "Achieving School Failure," discussing how some children are automatically placed in "pariah groups" by themselves and by their teachers. For a summary of my own views on the social organization of classrooms, see Smith (1989).

Renuce, Phillips, & Quartaro (1988) have proposed that instead of emulating the constrictive hypothetico-deductive research technology of physics, psychological theorists (such as cognitive scientists) should turn to more descriptive sciences like astronomy and zoology. They urge the employment of *grounded theory*, emphasizing the plausibility, comprehensiveness, and usefulness of explanations, rather than logical and experimental justifications.

For a relatively uncomplicated framework for beginning to analyze the social currents and controls of education, see Clarke (1989), and for a helpful examination of how teachers can come to understand and control their classrooms, see Strickland (1988) and other articles in the same journal issue. Changes in the role of teachers and their relationships to their students over the past century are discussed in Cuban (1984a). Mayher (1990) criticizes the "common sense" of education, particularly with respect to testing.

Urbanski (1988) provides a dramatic description of how teachers in one school district, led by their professional association, sought and gained greater empowerment in governing and changing their schools, based on the philosophy that "schools must be restructured as centers of inquiry and reflection—not of unexamined tradition."

5. Piaget's view was that the proper aims of education should be moral and intellectual autonomy, neither of which can be attained by instruction or information, but only by demonstration and engagement. For a clear summary, see Kamii (1984).

REFERENCES

Anderson, John A. (1989). A theory of the origins of human knowledge. *Artificial Intelligence, 40*, 312–351.

Attneave, Fred. (1974). How do you know? *American Psychologist, 29*, 493–499.

Bartlett, Frederick C. (1932). *Remembering: A Study in Experimental and Social Psychology.* London: Cambridge University Press.

Bateson, Gregory. (1980). *Mind and Nature.* New York: Bantam Books.

Bellow, Saul. (1987). *More Die of Heartbreak.* New York: Viking.

Bereiter, Carl, & Marlene Scardamalia. (1982). From conversation to composition: The role of instruction in a developmental process. In Robert Glaser (Ed.), *Advances in Instructional Psychology* (Vol. 2). Hillsdale, NJ: Erlbaum.

Berthoff, Ann E. (1981). *The Making of Meaning.* Portsmouth, NH: Boynton/Cook.

Berthoff, Ann E. (Ed.). (1983). *Reclaiming the Imagination.* Portsmouth, NH: Boynton/Cook.

Berthoff, Ann E. (1984). Is teaching still possible? Writing, meaning and higher order reasoning. *College English, 46*, 743–755.

Beyer, Barry K. (1983). Common sense about teaching thinking skills. *Educational Leadership, 41*(3), 44–49.

Beyer, Barry K. (1985, April). Critical thinking: What is it? *Social Education*, pp. 270–276.

Black, Alison, Paul Freeman, & Phillip N. Johnson-Laird. (1986). Plausibility and the comprehension of text. *British Journal of Psychology, 77*(1), 51–62.

Bloom, Benjamin S. (Ed.). (1956). *Taxonomy of Educational Objectives. Handbook I: Cognitive Domain.* New York: McKay.

Bloome, David, Pamela Puro, & Erine Theodorou. (1989). Procedural display and classroom lessons. *Curriculum Inquiry, 19*(3), 265–291.

Boorstin, Daniel J. (1985). *The Discoverers.* New York: Vintage.

Boring, Edwin G. (1957). *A History of Experimental Psychology* (2nd ed.). New York: Appleton-Century-Crofts.

Boulding, Kenneth E. (1981). Human knowledge as a special system. *Behavioral Science, 26*, 93–102.

Bradburn, Norman M., Lance J. Rips, & Steven K. Shevell. (1987). Answering autobiographical questions: The impact of memory and inference on surveys. *Science, 236*, 157–162.

Bransford, John D., & Barry S. Stein. (1984). *The IDEAL Problem Solver: A Guide for Improving Thinking, Learning and Creativity*. New York: Freeman.

Bransford, John D., Barry S. Stein, & Nancy J. Vye. (1982). Helping students learn how to learn from written texts. In M. H. Singer (Ed.), *Competent Reader, Disabled Reader*. Hillsdale, NJ: Erlbaum.

Bronowski, Jacob. (1978). *The Origins of Knowledge and Imagination*. New Haven, CT: Yale University Press.

Brown, Ann L. (1985). Mental orthopedics, the training of cognitive skills: An interview with Alfred Binet. In Susan F. Chipman, Judith W. Segal, & Robert Glaser (Eds.), *Thinking and Learning Skills* (Vol. 2). Hillsdale, NJ: Erlbaum.

Brown, Ann L., & Roberta A. Ferrara. (1985). Diagnosing zones of proximal development. In J. S. Wertsch (Ed.), *Culture, Communication and Development*. New York: Cambridge University Press.

Bruner, Jerome S. (1973). *Beyond the Information Given* (collected papers). New York: Norton.

Bruner, Jerome S. (1986). *Actual Minds, Possible Worlds*. Cambridge, MA: Harvard University Press.

Bruner, Jerome S., Jacqueline J. Goodenow, & George A. Austin. (1956). *A Study of Thinking*. New York: Wiley.

Bruner, Jerome S., & H. Haste. (Eds.). (1987). *Making Sense: The Child's Construction of the World*. London: Methuen.

Butler, Chris S. (1989). Systemic models: Unity, diversity and change. *Word*, *40*(1/2), 1–36.

Calkins, Lucy. (1980). When children want to punctuate: Basic skills belong in context. *Language Arts*, 57, 567–573.

Cameron, Donald. (1960). Blind variation and selective retention in creative thought as in other knowledge processes. *Psychological Review*, 67, 380–400.

Campbell, Joseph. (1949). *The Hero with a Thousand Faces*. New York: Pantheon.

Canetti, Elias. (1973). *Crowds and Power*. Harmondsworth, England: Penguin.

Carey, Susan. (1978). The child as word learner. In Morris Halle, J. Breslin, & George A. Miller (Eds.), *Linguistic Theory and Psychological Reality*. Cambridge, MA: MIT Press.

Chipman, Susan F., Judith W. Segal, & Robert Glaser. (Eds.). (1985). *Thinking and Learning Skills* (Vol. 2). Hillsdale, NJ: Erlbaum.

Chomsky, Noam. (1972). *Language and Mind*. New York: Harcourt.

Clarke, Mark A. (1989). Negotiating agendas: Preliminary considerations. *Language Arts*, 66, 370–380.

Coles, Robert. (1986a). *The Moral Life of Children*. Boston: Atlantic Monthly Press.

Coles, Robert. (1986b). *The Political Life of Children*. Boston: Atlantic Monthly Press.

Covino, William A. (1988). *The Art of Wondering*. Portsmouth, NH: Boynton/ Cook.

Cuban, Larry. (1984a). *How Teachers Taught: Constancy and Change in American Classrooms, 1890–1980*. New York: Academic Press.

Cuban, Larry. (1984b). Policy and research dilemmas in the teaching of reasoning: Unplanned designs. *Review of Educational Research, 54*(4), 655–681.

Cummins, Jim. (1989). *Empowering Minority Students*. Sacramento: California Association for Bilingual Education.

D'Angelo, Edward. (1971). *The Teaching of Critical Thinking*. Amsterdam: Gruner.

Dasser, Verena, Ib Ulbaek, & David Premack. (1989). The perception of intention. *Science, 243*, 365–367.

de Bono, Edward. (1976). *Teaching Thinking*. London: Penguin.

de Groot, A. D. (1965). *Thought and Choice in Chess*. The Hague: Mouton.

Dewey, John. (1910). *How We Think*. Boston: Heath.

Donaldson, Margaret. (1978). *Children's Minds*. London: Fontana.

Dressel, Paul I., & Lewis B. Mayhew. (1954). *Critical Thinking in Social Science*. Dubuque, IA: Brown.

Dreyfus, Hubert L., & Stuart E. Dreyfus. (1986). *Mind Over Machine*. New York: Free Press.

Eagleton, Terry. (1983). *Literary Theory*. Minneapolis: University of Minnesota Press.

Eckhoff, Barbara. (1983). How reading affects children's writing. *Language Arts, 60*(5), 607–616.

Egan, Kieran. (1989). *Teaching as Story Telling*. Chicago: University of Chicago Press.

Elley, Warwick B. (1989). Vocabulary acquisition from listening to stories. *Reading Research Quarterly, 24*(2), 174–187.

Ennis, Robert H. (1962). A concept of critical thinking. *Harvard Educational Review, 32*(1), 82–83.

Finocchiaro, Maurice F. (1981). Fallacies and the evaluation of reasoning. *American Philosophical Quarterly, 18*, 13–22.

Flavell, John H. (1963). *The Developmental Psychology of Jean Piaget*. New York: Van Nostrand.

Fodor, Jerry A. (1975). *The Language of Thought*. New York: Crowell.

Fodor, Jerry A. (1978). Propositional attitudes. *Monist, 61*, 501–523.

Fodor, Jerry A., & Zenon W. Pylyshyn. (1988). Connectionism and cognitive architecture: A critical analysis. *Cognition, 28*, 3–71.

Fraser, Dorothy McClure, & Edith West. (1961). *Social Studies in Secondary Schools*. New York: Ronald.

Frey, Peter W. (1986, November). A bit-mapped classifier. *BYTE, 11*(12), 161–172.

Frijda, Nico H. (1988). The laws of emotion. *American Psychologist, 43*, 349–358.

Frye, Northrop. (1963). *The Educated Imagination*. Toronto: Canadian Broadcasting Corporation.

Gadamer, Hans-Georg. (1975). *Truth and Method*. London: Sheed and Ward.

Gardner, Howard. (1982). *Art, Mind and Brain*. New York: Basic Books.

Gardner, Howard. (1983). *Frames of Mind*. New York: Basic Books.

Garrod, Simon, & Anthony Anderson. (1987). Saying what you mean in dialogue. *Cognition, 27*, 181–218.

Gazzaniga, Michael S. (1989). Organization of the human brain. *Science, 245*, 947–952.

Gellatly, Angus. (Ed.). (1986). *The Skillful Mind*. Milton Keynes, England: Open University.

Gelman, Rochel. (1979). Preschool thought. *American Psychologist, 34*, 900–911.

Gilhooly, K. J. (1982). *Thinking: Directed, Undirected and Creative*. London: Academic Press.

Giroux, Henry A. (1988). *Schooling and the Struggle for Public Life: Critical Pedagogy in the Modern Age*. Minneapolis: University of Minnesota Press.

Goelman, Hillel, Antoinette A. Oberg, & Frank Smith. (Eds.). (1984). *Awakening to Literacy*. Exeter, NH: Heinemann Educational Books.

Goodlad, John. (1984). *A Place Called School: Prospects for the Future*. New York: McGraw-Hill.

Greene, Maxine. (1988). Research currents: What are the language arts for? *Language Arts, 65* (5), 474–480.

Habermas, Jürgen. (1987). *The Philosophical Discourse of Modernity*. Cambridge, MA: MIT Press.

Halliday, Michael A. K. (1973). *Explorations in the Functions of Language*. London: Arnold.

Halpern, Diane F. (1984). *Thought and Knowledge: An Introduction to Critical Thinking*. Hillsdale, NJ: Erlbaum.

Hansen, Jane. (1981). The effects of inference training and practice on young children's reading comprehension. *Reading Research Quarterly, 3*, 391–417.

Hare-Mustin, Rachel T., & Jeanne Marecek. (1988). The meaning of difference: Gender theory, postmodernism and psychology. *American Psychologist, 43*, 455–464.

Heath, Shirley Brice. (1983). *Ways With Words*. Cambridge, England: Cambridge University Press.

Heath, Shirley Brice. (1985). Being literate in America: A sociohistorical perspective. In Jerome A. Niles & Rosary V. Lalik (Eds.), *Issues in Literacy: A Research Perspective* (Thirty-fourth Yearbook of the National Reading Conference). Rochester, NY: National Reading Conference.

Henle, Mary. (1962). On the relation between logic and thinking. *Psychological Review, 69*, 366–378.

Herrnstein, Richard J., R. S. Nickerson, M. de Sanchez, & J. A. Swets. (1986). Teaching thinking skills. *American Psychologist, 41*, 1279–1289.

Herzog, Harold A. (1988). The moral status of mice. *American Psychologist, 43*, 473–474.

Hitchcock, David. (1983). *A Guide to Evaluating Information*. Toronto: Methuen.

Hobson, J. Allan. (1988). *The Dreaming Brain*. New York: Basic Books.

Holden, Constance. (1987). Academy helps army be all that it can be. *Science*, 238, 1501–1502.

Holt, John. (1976). *Instead of Education: Ways to Help People Do Things Better*. Boston: Holt Associates.

Holt, John. (1989). *Learning All the Time*. Reading, MA: Addison-Wesley.

Howard, Vernon A. (1982). *Artistry: The Work of Artists*. Indianapolis: Hackett.

Howe, Michael J. A. (1988). Intelligence as an explanation. *British Journal of Psychology*, 79, 349–360.

Illich, Ivan, & Barry Sanders. (1988). *ABC: The Alphabetization of the Popular Mind*. New York: Vintage.

Inhelder, Barbel, Denys de Caprona, & Angela Cornu-Wells. (Eds.). (1987). *Piaget Today*. London: Erlbaum.

Innis, Harold A. (1951). *The Bias of Communication*. Toronto: University of Toronto Press.

Iran-Nejad, Asghar. (1989). A nonconnectionist schema theory of understanding surprise-ending stories. *Discourse Processes*, 12, 127–148.

Johnson, Ralph H., & J. Anthony Blair. (1985). Informal logic: The past five years 1978–1983. *American Philosophical Quarterly*, 22(3), 181–196.

Johnson-Laird, Phillip N. (1983). *Mental Models*. Cambridge, MA: Harvard University Press.

Johnson-Laird, Phillip N., D. J. Hermann, & R. Chaffin. (1984). Only connections: A critique of semantic networks. *Psychological Bulletin*, 96(2), 292–315.

Kahane, Howard. (1976). *Logic and Contemporary Rhetoric*. Belmont, CA: Wadsworth.

Kahneman, Daniel, Paul Slovic, & Amos Tversky. (1982). *Judgment under Uncertainty*. Cambridge, England: Cambridge University Press.

Kamii, Constance. (1984). Autonomy: The aim of education envisioned by Piaget. *Phi Delta Kappan*, 65, 410–415.

Karp, Walter. (1985, June). Why Johnny can't think: The politics of bad schooling. *Harper's*, pp. 69–73.

Klahr, D., W. G. Chase, & E. A. Lovelace. (1983). Structure and process in alphabetic retrieval. *Journal of Experimental Psychology: Learning, Memory and Cognition*, 9, 462–477.

Knoblauch, C. H., & Lil Brannon. (1988). Knowing our knowledge: A phenomenological basis for teacher research. In Louise Z. Smith (Ed.), *Audits of Meaning: A Festscrift in Honor of Ann E. Berthoff*. Portsmouth, NH: Boynton/Cook.

Konner, Melvin. (1982). *The Tangled Web: Biological Constraints on the Human Spirit*. New York: Harper & Row.

Kosslyn, Stephen M. (1980). *Image and Mind*. Cambridge, MA: Harvard University Press.

Kosslyn, Stephen M. (1983). *Ghosts in the Mind's Machine*. New York: Norton.

Krashen, Stephen D. (1984). *Writing: Research, Theory and Applications*. New York: Pergamon.

Krashen, Stephen D. (1985). *The Input Hypothesis: Issues and Implications*. New York: Longman.

Kuhn, Deanna. (1989). Children and adults as intuitive scientists. *Psychological Review, 96*(4), 474–689.

Lakoff, George. (1987). *Women, Fire, and Dangerous Things: What Categories Reveal about the Mind*. Chicago: University of Chicago Press.

Langer, Suzanne K. (1951). *Philosophy in a New Key*. Cambridge, MA: Harvard University Press.

Lehman, Darrin R., Richard O. Lempert, & Richard E. Nisbett. (1988). The effects of graduate training on reasoning: Formal discipline and thinking about everyday-life events. *American Psychologist, 43*, 431–442.

Lenneberg, Eric. (1967). *Biological Foundations of Language*. New York: Wiley.

LePan, Don. (1989). *The Cognitive Revolution in Western Culture. Vol. 1: The Birth of Expectation*. London: Macmillan.

Lessing, Doris. (1986). *Prisons We Choose to Live Inside*. Toronto: CBC Enterprises.

Levin, Joel R., Linda K. Shriberg, & Jill K. Berry. (1983). A concrete strategy for remembering abstract prose. *American Educational Research Journal, 20*, 277–290.

Liebowitz, Jay. (1989). If there is artificial intelligence, is there such a thing as artificial stupidity? *SIGART Newsletter, 109*, 26–28.

Locke, John. (1924). *An Essay Concerning Human Understanding* (A. S. Pringle-Pattison, Ed.). Oxford: Clarendon Press. (Original work published 1690)

Long, Debra L., & Arthur C. Graesser. (1988). Wit and humor in discourse processing. *Discourse Processes, 11*, 35–60.

Long, Shirley A., Peter N. Winograd, & Connie A. Bridge. (1989). The effects of reader and text characteristics and imagery reported during and after reading. *Reading Research Quarterly, 24*(3), 353–372.

Luke, Carmen, Suzanne de Castell, & Allan Luke. (1983). Beyond criticism: The authority of the school text. *Curriculum Inquiry, 13*(2), 111–127.

Luria, Alexander R. (1976). *Cognitive Development: Its Cultural and Social Foundations*. Cambridge, MA: Harvard Educational Press.

MacKinnon, Donald W. (1962). The nature and nurture of creative talent. *American Psychologist, 17*, 484–495.

Mandler, Jean Matter. (1984). *Stories, Scripts, and Scenes: Aspects of Schema Theory*. Hillsdale, NJ: Erlbaum.

Mandler, Jean Matter, & George Mandler. (1964). *Thinking: From Association to Gestalt*. New York: Wiley.

Margolis, Howard. (1987). *Patterns, Thinking, and Cognition: A Theory of Judgment*. Chicago: University of Chicago Press.

Mayher, John S. (1990). *Uncommon Sense: Theoretical Practice in Language Education*. Portsmouth, NH: Boynton/Cook.

McDermott, R. P. (1974). Achieving school failure: An anthropological approach to illiteracy and social stratification. In George D. Spindler (Ed.),

Education and Cultural Process: Toward an Anthropology of Education. New York: Holt, Rinehart & Winston.

McGinn, Colin. (1989). Can we solve the mind-body problem? *Mind, 98,* 391, 349–366.

McLeod, Alex. (1986). Critical literacy: Taking control of our own lives. *Language Arts, 62,* 31–50.

McPeck, John E. (1981). *Critical Thinking and Education.* Oxford, England: Martin Robertson.

McPeck, John E. (1990). *Teaching Critical Thinking: Dialogue and Dialectic.* New York: Routledge.

Meek, Margaret, Aiden Warlow, & Griselda Barton. (Eds). (1977). *The Cool Web.* New York: Atheneum.

Milgram, Stanley. (1974). *Obedience to Authority: An Experimental View.* New York: Harper & Row.

Miller, George A. (1962). Some psychological studies of grammar. *American Psychologist, 17,* 748–762.

Miller, Jane. (1983). *Many Voices: Bilingualism, Culture and Education.* London: Routledge & Kegan Paul.

Moffett, James. (1968). *Teaching the Universe of Discourse.* Boston: Houghton Mifflin.

Moravec, Hans. (1988). *Mind Children: The Future of Robot and Human Intelligence.* Cambridge, MA: Harvard University Press.

Nagy, William E., Patricia A. Herman, & Richard C. Anderson. (1985). Learning words from context. *Reading Research Quarterly, 20*(2), 233–253.

Neisser, Ulric. (1983). Components of intelligence or steps in routine procedures? *Cognition, 15,* 189–197.

Neisser, Ulric, & Eugene Winograd. (1988). *Remembering Reconsidered: Ecological and Traditional Approaches to the Study of Memory.* New York: Cambridge University Press.

Nelson, Katherine. (1986). *Event Knowledge.* Hillsdale, NJ: Erlbaum.

Nicholson, Graeme. (1984). *Seeing and Perceiving.* Atlantic Highlands, NJ: Humanities.

Noble, Douglas D. (1989). Mental materiel: The militarization of learning and intelligence in U.S. education. In Les Levidow & Kevin Robins (Eds.), *Cyborg Worlds: The Making of the Military Information Society.* London: Free Association Press.

Olson, David R. (1989). *Making Up Your Mind.* Presidential address to the Canadian Psychological Association.

Olson, David R., & Nandita Babu. (1989). *Critical Thinking.* Paper presented at the Conference on Critical Thinking, Memorial University of Newfoundland.

Olson, David R., Nancy Torrance, & Angela Hildyard. (Eds.). (1985). *Literacy, Language, and Learning: The Nature and Consequences of Reading and Writing.* Cambridge, England: Cambridge University Press.

Ong, Walter. (1977). *Interfaces of the Word.* Ithaca, NY: Cornell University Press.

Ortony, Anthony. (Ed.). (1979). *Metaphor and Thought*. New York: Cambridge University Press.

Paivio, Allan. (1986). *Mental Representations: A Dual Coding Approach*. New York: Oxford University Press.

Palmer, Richard E. (1969). *Hermeneutics*. Evanston, IL: Northwestern University Press.

Paul, Richard W. (1985). The critical-thinking movement. *National Forum*, *65*(1), 2–3, 32.

Penrose, Roger. (1989). *The Emperor's New Mind: Concerning Computers, Minds, and the Laws of Physics*. Oxford, England: Oxford University Press.

Perkins, David N. (1981). *The Mind's Best Work*. Cambridge, MA: Harvard University Press.

Perkins, David N. (1985). Reasoning as imagination. *Interchange*, *16*(1), 14–26.

Piattelli-Palmarini, Massimo. (Ed.). (1980). *Language and Learning: The Debate between Jean Piaget and Noam Chomsky*. Cambridge, MA: Harvard University Press.

Polanyi, Michael. (1958). *Personal Knowledge*. Chicago: University of Chicago Press.

Popper, Karl R. (1976). *Unended Quest: An Intellectual Autobiography*. London: Fontana/Collins.

Postman, Neil. (1989, December). Learning by story. *Atlantic*, pp. 119–124.

Pribram, Karl H. (1971). *Languages of the Brain*. Englewood Cliffs, NJ: Prentice-Hall.

Pylyshyn, Zenon W. (1984). *Computation and Cognition: Toward a Foundation for Cognitive Science*. Cambridge, MA: MIT Press.

Quine, Willard van Orman. (1960). *Word and Object*. Cambridge, MA: MIT Press.

Quinn, Paul C. (1987). The categorical representation of visual pattern information by young infants. *Cognition*, *27*, 145–179.

Renuce, David L., Jeffrey R. Phillips, & Georgia K. Quartaro. (1988). Grounded theory: A promising approach to conceptualization in psychology. *Canadian Psychology*, *29*(2), 139–150.

Rescorla, Robert A. (1988). Pavlovian conditioning: It's not what you think it is. *American Psychologist*, *43*, 151–160.

Restle, Frank. (1971). Theory of serial pattern learning. *Psychological Review*, *77*, 481–495.

Robinson, Ian. (1975). *The New Grammarians' Funeral*. Cambridge, England: Cambridge University Press.

Rock, Irwin. (1983). *The Logic of Perception*. Cambridge, MA: MIT Press.

Roller, Cathy M. (1989). Classroom interactions patterns: Reflections of a stratified society. *Language Arts*, *66*(5), 492–500.

Rosch, Eleanor, & B. B. Lloyd. (1978). *Cognition and Categorization*. Hillsdale, NJ: Erlbaum.

Rosen, Harold. (1986). The importance of story. *Language Arts*, *63*(3), 226–237.

Rosen, Harold. (1988). Stories of stories: Footnotes on sly gossipy practices. In Martin Lightfoot & Nancy Martin (Eds.), *The Word for Teaching Is Learning*. Portsmouth, NH: Heinemann Educational Books.

Rosenblatt, Louise M. (1978). *The Reader: The Text: The Poem*. Carbondale: Southern Illinois University Press.

Ryle, Gilbert. (1949). *The Concept of Mind*. London: Hutchinson.

Schank, Roger B. (1982). *Reading and Understanding: Teaching from the Perspective of Artificial Intelligence*. Hillsdale, NJ: Erlbaum.

Scribner, Sylvia, & Michael Cole. (1981). *The Psychology of Literacy*. Cambridge, MA: Harvard University Press.

Searle, John. (1983). *Intentionality: An Essay in the Philosophy of Mind*. Cambridge, England: Cambridge University Press.

Searle, John. (1984). *Minds, Brains and Science*. London: Penguin.

Segal, Judith W., Susan F. Chipman, & Robert Glaser. (Eds.). (1985). *Thinking and Learning Skills* (Vol. 1). Hillsdale, NJ: Erlbaum.

Shannon, Patrick. (1985). Reading instruction and social class. *Language Arts, 62*, 604–613.

Shannon, Patrick. (1989). The struggle for control of literacy lessons. *Language Arts, 6* (66), 625–634.

Shannon, Patrick, & David E. Fernie. (1985). Print and television: Children's use of the medium is the message. *The Elementary School Journal, 85* (5), 663–672.

Sheikh, Anees A. (Ed.). (1983). *Imagery: Current Theory, Research and Application*. New York: Wiley.

Simonton, Dean Keith. (1988). *Scientific Genius: A Psychology of Science*. Cambridge, England: Cambridge University Press.

Skvorecky, Josef. (1977). *The Engineer of Human Souls*. Don Mills, ON: Totem.

Smith, Frank. (1983a). Reading like a writer. *Language Arts, 60* (5), 558–567; reprinted in Smith, 1988a.

Smith, Frank. (1983b). *Essays Into Literacy*. Portsmouth, NH: Heinemann Educational Books.

Smith, Frank. (1985). In quest of creativity: Essay review. *Interchange, 16* (1), 120–126.

Smith, Frank. (1986). *Insult to Intelligence*. New York: Arbor House.

Smith, Frank. (1988a). *Joining the Literacy Club*. Portsmouth, NH: Heinemann Educational Books.

Smith, Frank. (1988b). *Understanding Reading* (4th ed.). Hillsdale, NJ: Erlbaum.

Smith, Frank. (1989). *How Schools Must Change*. Victoria, BC: Abel Press.

Smith, Louise Z. (Ed). (1988). *Audits of Meaning: A Festscrift in Honor of Ann E. Berthoff*. Portsmouth, NH: Boynton/Cook.

Smith, Mary K. (1941). Measurement of the size of general English vocabulary through the elementary grades and high school. *Genetic Psychology Monographs, 24*, 311–345.

Spindler, George D. (Ed.). (1974). *Education and Cultural Process: Toward an Anthropology of Education*. New York: Holt, Rinehart & Winston.

Spindler, George D. (Ed.). (1982). *Doing the Ethnography of Schooling: Educational Anthropology in Action.* New York: Holt, Rinehart & Winston.

Stanford, W. B. (1968). *The Ulysses Theme.* (2nd ed.). Ann Arbor: University of Michigan Press.

Stanovich, Keith, & Richard F. West. (1989). Exposure to print and orthographic processing. *Reading Research Quarterly, 24*(4), 402–433.

Staw, Barry M., & Jerry Ross. (1989). Understanding behavior in escalation situations. *Science, 246,* 216–220.

Sternberg, Robert J. (1983). Components of human cognition. *Cognition, 15,* 1–48.

Sternberg, Robert J. (1985). Human intelligence: The model is the message. *Science, 230,* 1111–1118.

Sternberg, Robert J. (1988). *The Triarchic Mind: A New Theory of Human Intelligence.* New York: Viking/Penguin.

Sternberg, Robert J., & Kastoor Bhana. (1986, October). Synthesis of research on the effectiveness of intellectual skills programs: Snake-oil remedies or miracle cures? *Educational Leadership,* pp. 61–67.

Stillings, Neil A., Mark A. Feinstein, Jay L. Garfield, Edwina L. Rissland, David A. Rosenbaum, Steven Weisler, & Lynne Baker-Ward. (1987). *Cognitive Science: An Introduction.* Cambridge, MA: MIT Press (Bradford Books).

Stock, Brian. (1983). *The Implications of Literacy.* Princeton, NJ: Princeton University Press.

Strickland, Dorothy S. (1988). The teacher as researcher: Toward the extended professional. *Language Arts, 65*(8), 754–764.

Suchman, Lucy A. (1987). *Plans and Situated Actions: The Problem of Human-Machine Communication.* Cambridge, England: Cambridge University Press.

Sulzby, Elizabeth. (1985). Children's emergent reading of favorite story books. *Reading Research Quarterly, 20*(4), 458–481.

Tierney, Robert J., Anna Soter, John F. O'Flahavan, & William McGinley. (1989). The effects of reading and writing upon thinking critically. *Reading Research Quarterly, 24*(2), 134–173.

Tulving, Endel. (1985a). How many memory systems are there? *American Psychologist, 40,* 385–398.

Tulving, Endel. (1985b). Memory and consciousness. *Canadian Journal of Psychology, 25,* 1–12.

Urbanski, Adam. (1988, November). The Rochester contract: A status report. *Educational Leadership,* pp. 48–52.

van Dongen, Richard. (1987). Children's narrative thought, at home and at school. *Language Arts, 64*(1), 79–87.

Vygotsky, Lev S. (1962). *Language and Thought.* Cambridge, MA: MIT Press.

Vygotsky, Lev S. (1978). *Mind in Society: The Development of Higher Psychological Processes.* Cambridge, MA: Harvard University Press.

Waitley, Denis. (1983). *Seeds of Greatness.* New York: Pocket Books.

Waldrop, M. Mitchell. (1987). Causality, structure, and common sense. *Science, 237,* 1297–1299.

Walkerdine, Valerie. (1982). From context to text: A psychosemiotic approach to abstract thought. In Michael Beveridge (Ed.), *Children Thinking Through Language.* London: Arnold.

Walkerdine, Valerie. (1985). *Language, Gender and Childhood.* London: Routledge & Kegan Paul.

Watson, Goodwin, & Edward M. Glaser. (1980). *Watson-Glaser Critical Thinking Appraisal Manual.* New York: Harcourt Brace Jovanovich.

Watt, W. C. (1989). Getting writing right. *Semiotica, 75* (3/4), 279–315.

Wendler, David, S. Jay Samuels, & Vienna K. Moore. (1989). The comprehension instruction of award-winning teachers, teachers with master's degrees, and other teachers. *Reading Research Quarterly, 24* (4), 382–401.

Whorf, Benjamin Lee. (1956). *Language, Thought and Reality.* New York: Wiley.

Wimmer, Heinz, & Josef Perner. (1983). Beliefs about beliefs: Representation and constraining function of wrong beliefs in children's understanding of deception. *Cognition, 13,* 103–128.

Wittgenstein, Ludwig. (1958). *The Blue and Brown Books.* New York: Harper.

Wong, Bernice Y. L. (1980). Activating the inactive learner. *Learning Disabilities Quarterly, 3,* 29–37.

Wong, Bernice Y. L. (1989). Musing about cognitive strategy training. *Intelligence, 13,* 1–4.

Yates, Frances A. (1966). *The Art of Memory.* London: Routledge & Kegan Paul.

INDEXES

SUBJECT INDEX

(Page numbers in *italics* are in Notes)
Algorithms 7
Ambiguity, 111, *154*
Analyzing/synthesizing, 25
Argumentation, *159*
Art, 48-49, 72-90
  creation of, 82-86
  sensitivity to, 79-81
  use of term, 76-77
Artificial intelligence, *137*, *151*
Artists, 82-86
Associationism, *139*
Athletics, 52
Authority (to think critically), 105, *160-61*

Bit-mapped classifiers, *146*
Bohr, Nils, *148*
Books, 126, 128
Brain, 45-47, 56, 88, 120-23, *138*, *144*, *157*
  and language, 117-18

Categories, *146*, *154*
Chaos, 55, 60, *145*
Charity, 20
Children, 51, 132, *141*, *143*, *148*, *153*, *158-61*
Cognitive science, 7, *136-38*, *151-52*, *158*
  alternatives, *160*
Cognitive structures, 7
Cognitive psychology, 7
Common sense, 22, 60-61, *137*
Communication, 112-13, *153-54*
Comprehension. *See* understanding
Computers, 7, 22, 57, 70, *136-38*, *146*
  and art, 89-90
Concept learning, 25
Confusion, 35-36
Constructivism, *154*
Creating reality, 45-49, *143*
Creative thinking, 72-90, *148-50*
  vs. critical thinking, 101-102
  see also thinking

Creativeness, 76-77, 83-86
  achieving, 86-88
  failure, 89
  language of, 73
Critical thinking, 91-107, *150-52*
  and language, 106-107
  language of, 91-98
  learning, 102-107
  "skills," 95-98
  vs. creative thinking, 101-102
  see also Thinking
Crowds, *158*
Culture, 39, 49, 63, 67, 132

Daydreaming, 45
Decisions, 15-17
Deconstructionism, *154*
Definitions, *153-54*
  vs. descriptions, 93
Darwin, Charles, *148*, *149*
Dispositions, 104-105
Doubt, 104, 129, *155*
Dreams, *143*
Dynamo of the brain, 53-55

Editing, 84
Education, 121-22, 124-33, *152*, *158-61*
  aims, *161*
  and research, *158*
  language of, *158*
Einstein, Albert, *149*
Emotions, 51, 79-80, *138*
  and music, 68
Ethnography, *159*, *160-61*
Events, 62, *147-48*
Exercise, *136*
Expectations, *144*, *155-56*
Experience, 124-25, *158-61*
Experimental psychology, 40-42, *141*, *142-43*

Face recognition, 56
Fact vs. opinion, 98-99, 130, *150*
Fantasy, 45, 46, 63
Feature analysis, 57-58, 59-60
Feelings. *See* emotions
Forgetting, 42
Freud, Sigmund, *148*
Functions vs. uses, 108, *153*

Galileo, 105
Games, 70
Generation of alternatives, 84, 101
Genius, *149-50*
Gossip, 64
Grammar, 39, *156*

Habit, 29-30, *145, 146*
Heisenberg, Werner, *148*
Hemispheric dominance, 121
Heuristics, 7
"Higher mental processes," 7
Humor, *154-55*

IDEAL, *151*
Imagery, *144, 150, 156*
Imagination, 45-54, *143-45*
  lack of, 53
  vs. communication, 112-13
Induction/deduction, 25
Informal logic. *See* logic
Information processing, 7, 12, 47, *136-37*,
  145
Information vs. experience, 47, 112
Inspiration, 84
Instruction. *See* teaching, education
Intelligence, 10, *139, 149, 152*
Intentions, 14, 21, 52, 63, 75, *138*
Interest, 127-28

Jesus, 105
Judgment, 99-101

Kitsch, *138*
Knowledge, 12, 102-103, 129, *137-39, 144,*
  145-46, 150

Language, 39, 49, 108-109, 110-15, *153-57*
  abstract vs. concrete, 117
  biological basis of, 153
  deep vs. surface structure, 116-17
  "in the head," 117-18

and reality, 115
and stories, 112-15
spoken vs. written, 111, *155-56*
and thought, 115-18
uses of, 110-12
Learning, 37, 51
  easy and difficult, 40
  to think, 124-33
Learning styles, 121, *157-58*
Leonardo da Vinci, 81
Letter recognition, 57-58, *148*
Linguistics, *156*
Literacy, 65, 115, *155-56, 160*
Literature, 48, 76-77
Logic, 21-23, *140-41, 145-46*
Luck, 81

Mathematics, 69
Memory. *See* remembering
Mental states, *155*
Metacognition, 26, 120, *141-42, 152*
Metaphor, 113, *144, 146, 154*
Mice, *138*
Michelangelo, 81
Mind and brain, 9-10, *155, 158*
Minority groups, 131, *158*
Mistakes, 29
Motivation. *See* intentions
Movement, 62, 69-70
Mozart, Wolfgang Amadeus, *148*
Music, 61, 66-69, 85
Myth, 65, *148*

Narrative. *See* stories
Neuroscience, 120-23, *146, 157*
Nonsense learning, 41

OMSITOG, *151*
Originality, 74-75

Painting, 84
Parallel distributed processes, *138*
Past, present, and future, 43, 46, 51, 64
Pasteur, Louis, *149*
Pattern-recognition, 55-71, *138, 145-48*
Performatives, 115, *155*
Play, *144, 150*
Power, *159-60*
Practice, *136*
Precision vs. clarity, 111
Prediction, 51. *See also* expectations

Presuppositions, 4, 32
Problem solving, 17-19, 52, *145, 151-52*
"Processes," 7, 8

Quality, 73-74
Questions, 130, *144*

Reading, 47
Reasoning, 19-21, *140, 148*
Relativity hypotheses, 116
Remembering, 50, *142-43, 148*
Respect, 127
Russian peasants, 22

Schemes, 7, *146*
Schubert, Franz, 74
"Science," *137*
Schools, 125
Selection among alternatives, 84, 101
Sense, 23
   of fitness, 65
   of ridiculous, 65
Sensory deprivation, 47
Shakespeare, William, *155*
Skills, 6, 21, 92-98, 130, *136*
Smell, 60
Socrates, 105
Songs, 67, 114
Specifications, 49-50, 58, *139*
   of artists, 84-86
Speech recognition, 59-60, *145*
Spreading activation, 7, *138*
Standards, 73-74
Stories, 62-66, 112-15, 131, *144, 145-48*
Story grammar, *147*
Strategies, *152*
Symbols, *149*

Talent, 87-88
Talking to ourselves, 45, 119, *156*
Taste, 60
Teaching, 127-33, *148, 151-52. See also* education
Tests, 106, *139*
Theories, *147*
"Things," 5
Thinking
   analyses of, 5-8
   and awareness, 13
   and children, 17, 21-22, *139*
   and education, 30, 124-33, *158-61*
   and imagination, 52-54
   and instruction, vii
   and language, 108-123, *139, 153-58*
   and learning, 42-44
   and perception, 15
   and remembering,, 35, 43-44
   and stories, 63-65
   and the brain, viii, 4, 7
   and understanding, 37, 43-44
   attitudes necessary for, 150
   "business of the brain," 9, 13-14
   by teachers, 131
   commonplace, 11, 12-31
   contrived, 27-28
   creatively, 72-90, *148-50*
   critically, 91-107, *150-52, 159,*
   divergent, 83
   easy and difficult, 27-31
   "executive," 24
   facilitating, 126-28
   "great," 132
   "higher-order," 23-26, *141*
   improving, 129-31, *139, 151-52*
   interfering with, 128-29, *159*
   language of, viii, 1-8, *136*
   need for, 131-33
   personal factors in, 29-30
   private and social, 28-29
   reclusiveness of, 118-23
   seventy-seven words, 1-2
   what it does, 109
   wishful/rueful, 28
Thought. *See* thinking
Time, 61-62

Ulysses, *148*
Understanding, 35-37, 51, *138*
Unproductive behavior, *150-51*
U.S. Army, *157-58*

Value, 73-74
Values, 2, 131
van Gogh, Vincent, 74
Vision, 55-59
Vocabulary, 38, *143*

"Wetware," *138*
Writing, 126, 128

AUTHOR INDEX

Anderson, Anthony, 154
Anderson, John A., 137
Anderson, Richard C., 143, 159
Attneave, Fred, 136
Austin, George A., 144

Babu, Nandita, 155
Bartlett, Frederick C., 146
Barton, Griselda, 148
Bateson, Gregory, 148
Bellow, Saul, 138
Bereiter, Carl, 141
Berry, Jill K., 144
Berthoff, Ann E., 145, 148, 159
Beyer, Barry K., 92-92, 99-100, 152
Bhana, Kastoor, 152
Binet, Alfred, 152
Black, Alison, 65
Blair, J. Anthony, 20, 140
Bloom, Benjamin S., 141
Bloome, David, 159
Boorstin, Daniel J., 49, 104, 148
Boring, Edwin G., 136, 142, 143
Boulding, Kenneth E., 143
Bradburn, Norman M., 142
Brannon, Lil, 148
Bransford, John D., 141, 151
Bridge, Connie A., 144
Bronowski, Jacob, 145
Brown, Ann L., 141, 152
Bruner, Jerome S., 52, 144
Butler, Chris S., 157

Calkins, Lucy, 159
Cameron, Donald, 149
Campbell, Joseph, 65, 148
Canetti, Elias, 158
Carey, Susan, 143
Chaffin, R., 156
Chase, W. G., 145
Chipman, Susan F., 151
Chomsky, Noam, 116, 156
Clarke, Mark A., 160
Cole, Michael, 155
Coles, Robert, 141
Cornu-Wells, Angela, 143
Covino, William A., 104, 144
Cuban, Larry, 152, 161
Cummins, Jim, 158

D'Angelo, Edward, 150
Dasser, Verena, 145
de Bono, Edward, 151, 152
de Caprona, Denys, 143
de Castell, Suzanne, 160
de Groot, A. D., 142
de Sanchez, M., 152
Dewey, John, 152
Donaldson, Margaret, 141
Dressel, Paul I., 99
Dreyfus, Hubert L., 137
Dreyfus, Stuart E., 137

Eagleton, Terry, 160
Ebbinghaus, Herman, 41
Eckhoff, Barbara, 159
Egan, Kieran, 148
Elley, Warwick B., 143
Engelhart, Max D., 141
Ennis, Robert H., 96-98, 99

Fernie, David E., 151
Ferrara, Roberta A., 141
Feuerstein, Reuven, 151, 152
Fillion, Bryant, 135
Finocchiaro, Maurice F., 141
Flavell, John H., 143
Fodor, Jerry A., 117, 138, 155
Fraser, Dorothy McClure, 99
Freeman, Paul, 65
Frey, Peter W., 146
Frijda, Nico H., 138
Frye, Northrop, 148
Furst, Edward J., 141

Gadamer, Hans-Georg, 160
Gardner, Howard, 144, 148, 149, 150
Garrod, Simon, 154
Gazzaniga, Michael S., 157
Gellatly, Angus, 139
Gelman, Rochel, 141
Gilhooly, K. J., 139
Giroux, Henry A., 159
Glaser, Edward M., 99
Glaser, Robert, 151
Goelman, Hillel, 160
Goodenow, Jacqueline J., 144
Goodlad, John, 159

Graesser, Arthur C., 155
Greene, Maxine, 159

Habermas, Jurgen, 140
Halliday, Michael A. K., 156
Halpern, Diane F., 152
Hansen, Jane, 144
Hardy, Barbara, 148
Hare-Mustin, Rachel T., 154
Haste, H., 144
Heath, Shirley Brice, 160
Henle, Mary, 140
Herman, Patricia A., 143, 159
Hermann, D. J., 156
Herrnstein, Richard J., 152
Herzog, Harold A., 138
Hildyard, Angela, 155
Hill, Walker H., 141
Hitchcock, David, 151
Hobson, J. Allan, 143
Holden, Constance, 157
Holt, John, 160
Howard, Vernon A., 73
Howe, Michael J. A., 149

Illich, Ivan, 153
Inhelder, Barbel, 143
Innis, Harold A., 155
Iran-Nejad, Asghar, 138

Johnson, Ralph H., 20, 140
Johnson-Laird, Phillip N., 65, 140, 156

Kahane, Howard, 141
Kahneman, Daniel, 145
Kamii, Constance, 161
Karp, Walter, 159
Klahr, D., 145
Knoblauch, C. H., 148
Konner, Melvin, 153
Kosslyn, Stephen M., 142
Krashen, Stephen D., 94, 141
Krathwohl, David R., 141
Kuhn, Deanna, 139

Lakoff, George, 154
Lehman, Darrin R., 152
Lempert, Richard O., 152
Lenneberg, Eric, 153
LePan, Don, 155
Lessing, Doris, 159

Levin, Joel R., 144
Liebowitz, Jay, 137
Lloyd, B. B., 146
Locke, John, 140
Long, Debra L., 144
Long, Shirley A., 155
Lovelace, E. A., 145
Luke, Allan, 160
Luke, Carmen, 160
Luria, Alexander R., 22

MacKinnon, Donald W., 149
Mandler, George, 136, 140
Mandler, Jean Matter, 136, 140, 146
Marecek, Jeanne, 154
Margolis, Howard, 140, 145, 150
Mayher, John S., 161
Mayhew, Lewis B., 99
McCune, George H., 99
McDermott, R. P., 160
McGinley, William, 159
McGinn, Colin, 158
McLeod, Alex, 160
McPeck, John E., 102-104, 152
Meek, Margaret, 148
Milgram, Stanley, 150
Miller, George A., 116
Miller, Jane, 144
Moffett, James, 148
Moore, Vienna K., 159
Moravec, Hans, 46, 137
Morse, Horace T., 99

Nagy, William E., 143, 159
Neisser, Ulric, 139, 142
Nelson, Katherine, 147
Nicholson, Graeme, 139
Nickerson, R. S., 152
Nisbett, Richard E., 152
Noble, Douglas D., 158

O'Flahavan, John F., 159
Oberg, Antoinette A., 160
Olson, David R., 155
Ong, Walter, 155
Ortony, Anthony, 144

Paivio, Allan, 144
Palmer, Richard E., 160
Paul, Richard W., 152
Pavlov, Ivan P., 146

Penrose, Roger, 137
Perkins, David N., 52, 73, 140, 144, 148, 149
Perner, Josef, 141
Phillips, Jeffrey R., 160
Piaget, Jean, 143, 156
Piattelli-Palmarini, Massimo, 156
Polanyi, Michael, 138, 145
Popper, Karl R., 9, 111
Postman, Neil, 148
Premack, David, 145
Pribram, Karl H., 118
Puro, Pamela, 159
Pylyshyn, Zenon W., 138, 155

Quartaro, Georgia K., 160
Quine, Willard van Orman, 136, 155
Quinn, Paul C., 141

Renuce, David L., 160
Rescorla, Robert A., 147
Restle, Frank, 145
Rips, Lance J., 142
Robinson, Ian, 156
Rock, Irwin, 139
Roller, Cathy M., 160
Rosch, Eleanor, 146
Rosen, Harold, 148
Rosenblatt, Louise M., 47
Ross, Jerry, 150
Ryle, Gilbert, 136, 155

Samuels, S. Jay, 159
Sanders, Barry, 153
Scardamalia, Marlene, 141
Schank, Roger B., 151
Scribner, Sylvia, 155
Searle, John, 137, 155
Segal, Judith W., 151
Shannon, Patrick, 151, 160
Sheikh, Anees A., 144
Shevell, Steven K., 142
Shriberg, Linda K., 144
Simonton, Dean Keith, 149
Skvorecky, Josef, 159
Slovic, P., 145
Smith, Frank, 138, 139, 141, 145, 149, 157, 160

Smith, Louise Z., 148
Smith, Mary K., 143
Smith, Mary-Theresa, 135, 153
Soter, Anna, 159
Spindler, George D., 160
Stanford, W. B., 148
Stanovich, Keith, 159
Staw, Barry M., 150
Stein, Barry S., 141, 151
Sternberg, Robert J., 139, 141, 149, 152
Stillings, Neil A., 146
Stock, Brian, 155
Strickland, Dorothy S., 161
Suchman, Lucy A., 137
Sulzby, Elizabeth, 148
Swets, J. A., 152

Theodorou, Erine, 159
Tierney, Robert J., 159
Tolkien, J. R. R., 139
Torrance, Nancy, 155
Tulving, Endel, 142
Tversky, Amos, 145

Ulbaek, Ib, 145
Urbanski, Adam, 161

van Dongen, Richard, 148
Vye, Nancy J., 141
Vygotsky, Lev S., 143, 148, 155, 158

Waitley, Denis, 144
Waldrop, M. Mitchell, 137
Walkerdine, Valerie, 144, 160
Warlow, Aiden, 144
Watson, Goodwin, 99
Watt, W. C., 155
Wendler, David, 159
West, Edith, 99
West, Richard F., 159
Whorf, Benjamin Lee, 116
Wimmer, Heinz, 141
Winograd, Eugene, 142
Winograd, Peter N., 144
Wittgenstein, Ludwig, 136
Wong, Bernice Y. L., 144, 152

Yates, Frances A., 148

ABOUT THE AUTHOR

After early education in England, Frank Smith gained a first-class honors B.A. in cognitive psychology at the University of Western Australia and a Ph.D. in psycholinguistics at Harvard University. For fifteen years he was a professor of education at the Universities of Toronto and Victoria, and he is now a full-time writer, lecturer, and researcher, making his home in Victoria, British Columbia.